HORSERACING
A Guide to Profitable Betting

Peter May

Published by Raceform Ltd
High Street, Compton, Newbury, Berkshire, RG20 6NL
Raceform Ltd is a wholly-owned subsidiary of Trinity Mirror plc

A catalogue record for this book is available from the British Library.

ISBN 1-904317-42-1

Designed by Sam Pentin
Printed by Alden Press, Oxford

Contents

INTRODUCTION

Horseracing: A Guide To Profitable Betting does not adopt the format on the standard racing book with opening chapters providing a background to the sport and betting intricacies, following chapters expanding on an idea, then an evaluation section showing how well the method works. Instead this book presents a collection of articles covering different aspects of betting and form analysis.

Some of the chapters are expanded versions of articles previously published in magazines and newspapers such as Raceform Update, others are new items. Consequently this text can be used as a reference guide with the reader able to refer to a specific section of interest in order to gain an alternative view or a new idea for further research.

Essentially the book is divided into three sections: Race Analysis, Betting Strategies and Computer Modelling. The Race Analysis section focuses on the more general approaches to form analysis and includes chapters covering the effect of the draw, pedigree analysis and race profiling. Part two of the text covers Betting Strategies. In this section techniques are explored that can be used to improve betting returns such as methods designed to evaluate recent stable form, or approaches to system development.

Part three is devoted to computer modeling. In recent years computers have become more common place at home and as such their use with respect to betting has increased dramatically. The three articles in this section illustrate different computer-based methods for analysing races and include the use of artificial neural networks, a technology that is becoming increasingly more popular with racing enthusiasts.

The first chapter of the Race Analysis section concerns Race Profiling. Essentially this is an extension of race trend analyses which are generally published in the daily press before a major race. Individual race trends, though, are only valid for a small selection of the top races which have their own characteristics. One Class E handicap hurdle race is very much like another, so extracting the details for a particular handicap hurdle race run at Exeter in November may not be that informative or reliable. However, given the degree of similarity between these events it is possible to analyse all similar races to generate a profile of the likely winner based on a large sample. For instance when considering a 3m3f handicap hurdle race at Sedgefield it may be helpful to find the profile of the most likely winner of all long distance hurdle races. And given the amount of data available, this could be further restricted to a similar field size, the same race class, or to races run on a similar surface or a similar track. Methods for generating general race profiles, as well as a collection of profiles for Jumps and Flat racing is detailed in this chapter.

The effect of weight carried by horses is often debated in the racing press. The second chapter in the Race Analysis section covers this topic and a method for calculating the degree of the effect is illustrated using the Lingfield All Weather course as a case study.

Draw biases are often discussed before and after flat races. A poor draw can effectively reduce the chance of a horse winning to zero, whereas a good draw, at some tracks, can give even the most unlikely winner a chance of success. In Assessing and Exploiting the Effect of the Draw (an updated version of an article first published in *Raceform Update* in 2002), a method is presented that can be used to determine the draw effect at every course. Whilst knowing the effect of the draw is an important aspect of analysing flat races, for computer modeling it is necessary to quantify the effect. This is also covered in Chapter 3 along with an analysis of the best jockeys for sprint races and a list of tracks where the draw bias should be given the most consideration.

American Handicappers rely on the Dosage Profiles of horses in order to assess their pedigrees. There is no equivalent system this side of the Atlantic, but in Chapter 4 methods are proposed which provide the reader with pedigree profiles that indicate the likely levels of stamina and ability the progeny of a sire may possess. In contrast to the Dosage method, this simple approach requires just the sire and dam's sire in order to generate profiles which can be related directly to distance and ability without further interpretation. Detailed results from testing the approach on a sample of races are also given to provide a guide as to the best way of using this innovative approach.

Flat handicap races are far from easy to solve. Though the draw can be used for some tracks, an alternative approach is one of elimination. In Chapter 5 the details of elimination-based techniques are examined and a straightforward method proposed. This powerful method can be used to reduce a large field of runners to a more manageable set increasing the likelihood of finding the winner.

All Weather racing is increasing in popularity as the racing authorities appear to be favouring sand racing over Jumps racing. The competitive nature of the racing ensures the bookmakers' a good profit which in turn increases the revenue received by the industry. However, one of the main problems faced by the punter is assessing horses that are previously unraced on the surface. In Race Analysis 6: All Weather Debutants (an article first published in SmartSig Confidential in 2003) these runners are analysed and ability thresholds determined that separate the likely winners from the likely losers.

Section Two, Betting Strategies, opens with two updated articles covering the use of trainer information. These were first published in *Raceform Update* in 2002. Many trainers have fixed patterns for running horses. Some will always run their best juveniles, for instance, at a specific course at a certain time of year. An analysis of these trends can be very lucrative for the informed punter. In the first Trainer article these trends are listed for Flat and Jumps racing based on trainer, track and race type. Further analyses cover horses making their handicap debuts, and those returning from a long course absence. The second article focuses on recent stable form. Methods for evaluating whether a stable is in form are detailed and the results of such methods examined.

Owners and Jockeys are added to the trainer analyses in the third chapter of Betting Strategies section. Whilst many punters will be familiar with certain trainer and jockey combinations, little research has been devoted to owner analyses. A selection of profitable "Trainer-Owner-Jockey" combinations is presented in this article, which are sub-divided by race type and may continue to be profitable over the coming seasons.

Win betting is a popular option for many punters but there are occasions when it is beneficial to bet each way. And these are not just for the longer priced horses. In Win and Each Way Betting (first published in *SmartSig Confidential* in 2003), these two types of bet are examined from theoretical and practical viewpoints and the results presented for different race types and field sizes. The each way option is then extended to cover each way doubles with a simulation illustrating the benefits of this approach.

A systematic approach to betting is very popular for horseracing followers, and the fifth chapter of the Betting Strategies section illustrates how a racing system can be developed using sensitivity analysis. The method is used in many different numerical disciplines and essentially monitors how one system reacts to changes to its influencing factors. Though such an approach can produce "over-fitted" systems that do not perform well in the future, several safeguards and tests are detailed which can be used to avoid this pitfall.

Part Two of the book ends with two chapters covering favourites to follow and claiming jockeys. The first presents analyses of the performance of favourites for Jumps and Flat racing and shows the type of favourite that has produced a profit in the past to the level stakes bettor. Claiming jockeys often form part of racing systems and in the seventh chapter of Betting Strategies analyses are presented which illustrate which claiming jockeys are worth following.

The final section of the book covers the use of computer-based forecasting systems. The traditional approach to computer system development is examined and alternatives using more effective technology, such as neural networks, are proposed and evaluated.

RACE ANALYSIS
CHAPTER 1: RACE PROFILING

There are almost as many ways to analyse a horserace as there are horses. Form-based approaches are probably the most popular, and the recent availability of race data on personal computers has promoted the use of systems and computer-based forecasting methods. However, another technique that appears to be increasing in popularity is Race Profiling.

Race Profiling

Unlike Form Study, race profiling does not attempt to quantify the ability of a horse. Instead it extracts the key characteristics of the race and uses these features to generate a profile of the most likely race winner. These profiles can have few or many attributes depending on the significance of the features and the depth of data supporting each one.

Some races do not lend themselves to profiling and it is difficult to find a reliable profile for the likely winner. This may be due to a lack of historical data, on which to base the profile, or simply that the race is won by a wide range of horses without favouring a specific type. However, many races have very exact profiles and are won on a regular basis by horses that exhibit a specific set of qualities.

The logic underlying the Race Profiling method concerns the dominance of horses with certain characteristics in specific races. Often races are won by a particular type of horse, with others having only a minimal chance. For instance, age is often a key factor. Jumps races are invariably won by the younger horses.

However, there are cases where a very narrow age range can be associated with a race. Under such circumstances the horses lying outside this range can be considered unlikely winners, and if one or more happens to be a short price, then it may be possible to return a good profit by not only backing the horses with positive traits, but by laying those animals possessing negative profiles.

Specific Race Profiles

Essentially there are two types of profile: a Specific Race Profile and a General Race Profile. The former is most commonly applied to the main races of the year in the form of five year- or ten year-trends. In order to generate a specific race profile the credentials of the recent winners of the race are examined and the key trends extracted. The specific race profile for the Hennessy Cognac Gold Cup provides a good example.

The "Hennessy" is run in late November at Newbury. Normally the ground is on the soft side, and this, combined with the fact that the race is run over 3m2f, makes it a thorough test of stamina. Although the race is a handicap it attracts potentially top class horses.

From Table 1 it can be seen that several common factors are associated with the majority of recent winners. For instance, the last 20 winners of this race were all aged between six and nine years old, and of the last ten winners only Suny Bay carried more than 11-00 in weight. Three of the last 20 winners were unraced in the current season, but the remaining 17 all finished in the frame on their run before Newbury. Galway Blaze ran third before winning the Hennessy, four others finished runner-up whist the other 12 all won. Furthermore all 17 ran in a handicap chase prior to the big race, with 12 starting first or second favourite. Given such strong trends forming the profile it is easy to reduce the field to a select few for more detailed analysis.

The Hennessy Gold Cup is not the only race for which the winners possess distinctive traits, many of the top races can be analysed in a similar fashion and informative trends deduced. Unfortunately this sample only constitutes a small proportion of the ever expanding pool of races run each season and an alternative approach is required for the other events.

One Class E handicap hurdle race, for instance, is very much like another, so extracting the details for a particular handicap hurdle race run at Exeter in November may not be that informative or reliable. However, given the degree of similarity between these less prominent events it is possible to analyse all similar races to generate a profile of the likely winner based on a large sample. For instance when considering a 3m3f handicap hurdle race at Sedgefield it may be helpful to find the profile of the most likely winner of all long distance hurdle races.

Given the amount of data available, this could be further restricted to a similar field size, the same race class, or to races run on a similar surface or a similar track. Consequently a more general approach is more applicable to the majority of races run each season.

The Hennessy Cognac Gold Cup

Year	Winning Horse	Trainer	Starting Price	Age	Weight Carried	BHB Rating	Rnrs	Latest Race in Current Season			
								Position	Starting Price	Distance	Race Type
2002	Be My Royal	W P Mullins	33/1	8	10-00	136	25	1	5/2F	3m4f	HcpChs
2001	What's Up Boys	P J Hobbs	14/1	7	10-12	145	14	Unraced in current season			
2000	King's Road	N Twiston-Davies	7/1	7	10-07	137	17	2	10/1²f	3m1½f	HcpChs
1999	Ever Blessed	M Pitman	9/2F	7	10-00	136	13	1	15/8F	3m	HcpChs
1998	Teton Mill	Miss V Williams	5/1²f	9	10-05	139	16	1	4/1	3m1½f	HcpChs
1997	Suny Bay	C P E Brooks	9/4F	8	11-08	162	14	1	10/3²f	3m	HcpChs
1996	Coome Hill	W W Dennis	11/2²f	7	10-00	136	11	1	2/1F	3m1½f	HcpChs
1995	Couldnt Be Better	C P E Brooks	15/2	8	10-08	147	11	1	11/8F	3m	HcpChs
1994	One Man	G Richards	4/1²f	6	10-00	130	16	1	4/9F	2m4f	HcpChs
1993	Cogent	A Turnell	10/1	9	10-01	145	9	2	6/1	3m	HcpChs
1992	Sibton Abbey	F Murphy	40/1	7	10-00	139	13	1	3/1²f	3m1f	HcpChs
1991	Chatam	M C Pipe	10/1	7	10-06	145	15	Unraced in current season			
1990	Arctic Call	O Sherwood	5/1²f	7	11-00	-	13	1	5/4²f	3m	HcpChs
1989	Ghofar	D R C Elsworth	5/1j²f	6	10-02	-	8	2	10/1	2m4f	HcpChs
1988	Strands Of Gold	M C Pipe	10/1	9	10-00	-	12	Unraced in current season			
1987	Playschool	D H Barons	6/1²f	9	10-08	-	12	2	4/1	3m	HcpChs
1986	Broadheath	P F Nicholls	6/1²f	9	10-05	-	15	1	4/1j²f	3m1f	HcpChs
1985	Galway Blaze	J G FitzGerald	11/2	9	10-00	-	15	3	10/1	3m	HcpChs
1984	Burrough Hill Lad	Mrs J Pitman	10/3F	8	12-00	-	13	1	1/4F	3m1f	HcpChs
1983	Brown Chamberlin	F T Winter	7/2F	8	11-08	-	12	1	4/5F	3m	HcpChs

General Race Profiles

General race profiles, as the title suggests, are based on a wide range of races, as opposed to a single event. It is possible to create a handicap chase profile, for instance, based on all such races run in a specific country. Whilst this is a very general profile it can be further restricted by the main discriminating factors such as race distance, going, time of year, race class and track. Using these additional inputs the profile can be structured to provide the information required based on the largest possible sample of races. Consequently it becomes more robust than a single race profile and hence more reliable.

The main advantage of general race profiles is their applicability. Few races can be profiled in isolation, whereas general profiles will apply to the remaining majority. Furthermore changing trends are more likely to be apparent from an analysis of several races as opposed to a single event. For instance, increased competitiveness in a specific sector of racing may reduce the proportion of events won by the favourite. When analysing a single race this may become obvious after a reasonable time period and number of races, but in a general profile it will be visible sooner, allowing the bettor to take advantage of the changing pattern and structure his/her bets accordingly.

A Selection of Jump Race Profiles

In this section a sample of general race profiles are examined in detail for the four main National Hunt race classifications: novices' hurdle races, novices' chases, handicap hurdle races and handicap chases. The profiles are based on the five seasons to end 2002/03. In each table the "Prop^n" column refers to the proportion of races won by the horses in each category. For instance in Table 1 it can be seen that 26% of races are won by horses aged five years old.

Novices' Hurdle Races

There are several types of novices' hurdle race. The following profiles apply to a standard novices' hurdles event, and exclude novices' claiming hurdle races, novices' selling hurdles and novices' handicap hurdles.

These races are restricted to the less experienced horses which can expect to progress to handicap hurdle races or to take the chasing route after gaining racing experience over hurdles. Consequently there is a significant bias with respect to the age of the winners. During the period of analysis, five and six-year-olds won over half of these races, with less than 5% being taken by horses aged eight or older. However, in terms of profit and loss, the figure remains reasonably constant to age six, then declines as the age of the horse increases. Over 60% of the winners that had been assessed by the BHB were rated in the 80-109 handicap range, though the horses rated between 100 and 119 returned the lowest deficit at starting price (about 4% of stake). Given the way these races are framed, the majority of winners carried less then 11 stone. A few were allotted 12-01 or more and these had an excellent success rate but returned a slight loss at starting price. Approximately 70% of the winners were priced at 4/1 or less. The outsiders, priced at 11/1 or higher, accounted for only 11% of victories and returned a huge loss based on a level stake bet at starting price. Horses that failed to complete on their latest start had a very poor follow-up record. Favourites, in contrast, did well and returned only a slight loss at starting price (approximately 2p/£1 staked).

Table 1: Novices' Hurdles Races by Age of Runner

Age	Prop[n]	Wins	Runs	Wins%	Average Ret/£1
3yo	11%	282	2986	9%	-£0.43
4yo	21%	558	5680	10%	-£0.46
5yo	26%	690	7246	10%	-£0.45
6yo	26%	680	6559	10%	-£0.44
7yo	12%	309	3733	8%	-£0.50
8yo	4%	96	1491	6%	-£0.55
9yo	1%	31	536	6%	-£0.62
10yo	0%	7	233	3%	-£0.68
11yo	0%	1	61	2%	-£0.95
12yo+	0%	1	55	2%	-£0.94

Table 2: Novices' Hurdle Races by Weight Carried

Weight Carried	Prop[n]	Wins	Runs	Wins%	Average Ret/£1
12-01+	0%	11	19	58%	-£0.03
11-8..12-00	10%	267	801	33%	-£0.09
11-0..11-07	30%	797	4700	17%	-£0.28
10-8..10-13	50%	1340	17065	8%	-£0.47
10-0..10-07	9%	239	5881	4%	-£0.65
..9-13	0%	1	114	1%	-£0.87

Table 3: Novices' Hurdle Races by Starting Price

Starting Price	Prop^n	Wins	Runs	Wins%	Average Ret/£1
Odds On	25%	670	1062	63%	-£0.02
Ev - 2/1	23%	608	1574	39%	-£0.03
9/4 - 4/1	21%	561	2503	22%	-£0.09
9/2 - 6/1	11%	288	1936	15%	-£0.07
13/2-10/1	9%	243	3043	8%	-£0.26
11/1-16/1	6%	154	3772	4%	-£0.40
18/1-33/1	4%	108	6571	2%	-£0.56
40/1+	1%	23	8119	0%	-£0.84

Table 4: Novices' Hurdle Races by Position on Last Run

Position on Latest Run	Prop^n	Wins	Runs	Wins%	Average Ret/£1
Won	28%	744	2410	31%	-£0.11
2nd or 3rd	29%	758	4419	17%	-£0.29
Unplaced	25%	677	12862	5%	-£0.52
Fell,BD,UR	3%	69	1026	7%	-£0.41
Pulled Up	3%	86	2861	3%	-£0.68
Ref/RanOut	0%	2	87	2%	-£0.95
CO/SlipUp	0%	1	23	4%	-£0.91
Unraced	12%	318	4892	7%	-£0.52

Restricting the sample to just Class A and B novices' hurdle races changes the profile significantly. Whilst the distribution of winners by starting price remains similar to the analysis of all race classes (though odds on shots show a profit of approximately 12p/£1) an analysis by finishing position on latest run unearths different results. For Class A and B races, 51% of winners over the five seasons had won their latest race, and a further 22% had been placed second or third.

Table 5: Class A and B Novices' Hurdle Races by Position on Last Run

Position on Latest Run	Prop[n]	Wins	Runs	Wins%	Average Ret/£1
Won	51%	91	504	18%	-£0.32
2nd or 3rd	22%	39	409	10%	-£0.40
Unplaced	14%	25	413	6%	-£0.44
Fell,BD,UR	2%	4	39	10%	-£0.37
Pulled Up	2%	3	49	6%	-£0.55
Unraced	8%	15	189	8%	-£0.62

Isolating the Class E-G races produces a different profile. In terms of ratings, horses with a handicap mark of between 80 and 109 accounted for 70% of races won by rated horses. However, a few higher rated horses are entered for these contests and they are worth following. In the past horses rated at 120 or higher produced an excellent success rate as well as returning a small profit.

Other factors can also affect the profile. For instance, taking all novices' hurdle races run over at least 3 miles on going softer than good produces some interesting results. Seven-year-olds took a higher proportion of races, about 28%, though six-year-olds still won the largest share. Favourites returned a small profit, and most interestingly horses that had previously won over the race distance returned a profit of 13p/£1. Weight did not seem to stop these horses either, with over half of the races going to horses carrying over 11 stone. And those burdened with 11-08 or more returned a healthy profit of 25p/£1.

Table 6: Soft ground Novices' Hurdle Races Over at Least 3 miles by Age of Runner

Age	Prop[n]	Wins	Runs	Wins%	Average Ret/£1
4yo	5%	7	69	10%	-£0.10
5yo	16%	22	265	8%	-£0.50
6yo	36%	48	400	12%	-£0.22
7yo	28%	38	279	14%	-£0.32
8yo	7%	10	166	6%	-£0.62
9yo	5%	7	61	12%	-£0.45
10yo	1%	2	29	7%	-£0.82
11yo	0%	0	7	0%	-£1.00
12yo+	0%	0	9	0%	-£1.00

Table 7: Soft ground Novices' Hurdle Races Over at Least 3 miles by Weight Carried

Weight Carried	Prop^n	Wins	Runs	Wins%	Average Ret/£1
12-01+	1%	1	1	100%	+£1.00
11-8..12-00	15%	20	47	43%	+£0.25
11-0..11-17	37%	49	304	16%	-£0.22
10-8..10-13	41%	55	668	8%	-£0.33
10-0..10-07	7%	9	265	3%	-£0.79

Novices' Chases

Horses can generally run in a novices' chase if they have not won a chase prior to the current season. Again this categorisation can include novices' handicap chases and novices' selling chases, though these are excluded from the following analyses.

The profile for novices' chases is similar to that for novices' hurdle races which is not too surprising given the similarity in the conditions, with the only significant difference being the size of the obstacles. With respect to age, six- and seven-year-olds won 55% of races run during the five seasons, and although four-year-olds only accounted for 1% of all victories, they did return an excellent profit at starting price, 68p/£1 in fact. The time between runs is often a good discriminating factor when analysing races, but for novices' chases the average return at starting price is reasonably consistent across the various "days since" categories, similarly the success rate. So even though a third of all winners had raced within 15 and 28 days previously, this is not a significant profiling factor. Starting price is a key element though. Three-quarters of all winners were priced at 4/1 or less, with odds on shots showing the smallest loss. Recent form is another important factor, over 60% of winners finished in the frame last time out, with horses that failed to complete on their latest run accounting for only 14% of races and returning a huge loss.

Table 8: Novices' Chases by Age of Runner

Age	Prop[n]	Wins	Runs	Wins%	Average Ret/£1
4yo	1%	23	93	25%	+£0.68
5yo	14%	257	1240	21%	-£0.16
6yo	26%	488	2985	16%	-£0.25
7yo	29%	531	3467	15%	-£0.23
8yo	19%	343	2834	12%	-£0.34
9yo	8%	146	1416	10%	-£0.48
10yo	3%	50	741	7%	-£0.59
11yo	1%	10	271	4%	-£0.85
12yo+	0%	4	126	3%	-£0.47

Table 9: Novices' Chases by Course Absence

Days Since Last Run	Prop[n]	Wins	Runs	Wins%	Average Ret/£1
1..7	4%	79	614	13%	-£0.29
8..14	17%	319	2366	14%	-£0.38
15..28	33%	606	3991	15%	-£0.29
29..60	21%	387	2430	16%	-£0.17
61..100	5%	90	677	13%	-£0.41
101+	18%	335	2637	13%	-£0.34
Unraced	2%	36	458	8%	-£0.52

Table 10: Novices' Chases by Position on Latest Run

Position on Latest Run	Prop[n]	Wins	Runs	Wins%	Average Ret/£1
Won	26%	490	1630	30%	-£0.13
2nd or 3rd	34%	634	3161	20%	-£0.13
Unplaced	24%	442	4760	9%	-£0.34
Fell,BD,UR	8%	141	1180	12%	-£0.40
Pulled Up	6%	107	1925	6%	-£0.54
Ref/RanOut	0%	2	45	4%	-£0.87
CO/SlipUp	0%	0	12	0%	-£1.00
Unraced	2%	36	460	8%	-£0.53

In general the favourite lost less than 1p for every £1 staked. However, the loss increased as the field size increased to a level of over 50p per £1 for races with 16 or more runners. Seven-year-olds did best in races over 3m2f or further accounting for a quarter of all victories, and previous distance winners showed a 9p/£1 profit at starting price.

Handicap Hurdle Races

Although most handicap hurdle races are open to all runners, there are a few exceptions such as novices' handicap hurdle races. The following analysis excludes these races as well as amateur handicaps, claiming handicaps and selling handicap hurdle races.

Five to seven year-olds dominate this race type, with horses aged over eight taking just 14% of races. Clearly the younger horses are the ones to consider. However, the most significant factor relates to the previous race. Horses that completed on their most recent start won over 93% of all handicap hurdle races. The others, though winning 7% of the time, returned a huge loss to punters and should be avoided.

With respect to starting price, the distribution of winners is more uniform than for the non-handicap races, with horses starting at 4/1 or under taking less than 50% of these events. Runners priced at more than 16/1 won approximately 4% of all races at a strike rate of about 1 in 50. In terms of profit, odds on shots were best, retuning a profit of about 10p for every £1 staked over the past five seasons.

Table 11: Handicap Hurdle Races by Position on Last Run

Position on Latest Run	Prop[n]	Wins	Runs	Wins%	Average Ret/£1
Won	25%	653	3590	18%	-£0.14
2nd or 3rd	29%	742	5797	13%	-£0.24
Unplaced	39%	1012	12226	8%	-£0.21
Fell,BD,UR	3%	74	1080	7%	-£0.51
Pulled Up	4%	106	2294	5%	-£0.44
Ref/RanOut	0%	4	80	5%	-£0.37
CO/SlipUp	0%	2	22	9%	-£0.41

Table 12: Handicap Hurdle Races by Starting Price

Starting Price	Prop[n]	Wins	Runs	Wins%	Average Ret/£1
Odds On	4%	107	172	62%	+£0.06
Ev - 2/1	15%	380	1105	34%	-£0.09
9/4 - 4/1	27%	711	3445	21%	-£0.14
9/2 - 6/1	18%	481	3499	14%	-£0.14
13/2-10/1	20%	514	5673	9%	-£0.17
11/1-16/1	11%	287	5351	5%	-£0.23
18/1-33/1	4%	116	4800	2%	-£0.41
40/1+	0%	5	1098	1%	-£0.77

Class A and B races were even better for odds on punters with the average profit doubled. And although the horses that failed to complete on their previous run took a slightly larger share of these races, 40% of races were won by horses that were successful most recently.

Table 13: Class A and B Handicap Hurdle Races by Starting Price

Starting Price	Prop[n]	Wins	Runs	Wins%	Average Ret/£1
Odds On	5%	13	20	65%	+£0.13
Ev - 2/1	14%	40	113	35%	-£0.06
9/4 - 4/1	24%	70	339	21%	-£0.15
9/2 - 6/1	15%	44	347	13%	-£0.19
13/2-10/1	22%	62	669	9%	-£0.14
11/1-16/1	13%	38	669	6%	-£0.18
18/1-33/1	7%	20	697	3%	-£0.29
40/1+	0%	0	172	0%	-£1.00

Handicap Chases

An analysis of handicap chases, without selling, claiming and novices' events, shows that eight-year-olds take the largest proportion of races, approximately 25%, with horses over the age of ten accounting for just 11% of victories.

Table 14: All Handicap Chases by Age of Runner

Age	Prop[n]	Wins	Runs	Wins%	Average Ret/£1
4yo	0%	0	2	0%	-£1.00
5yo	2%	53	373	14%	-£0.03
6yo	8%	238	1419	17%	+£0.03
7yo	19%	535	3495	15%	-£0.08
8yo	25%	732	5152	14%	-£0.13
9yo	22%	635	5209	12%	-£0.15
10yo	13%	365	3822	10%	-£0.21
11yo	7%	200	2345	9%	-£0.25
12yo+	4%	124	1740	7%	-£0.34

Though this profile holds true throughout the year, during the Summer months (May to August) the younger runners returned the best profit, with six-year-olds the horses to follow based on this statistic. Over the last few seasons these horses returned a profit exceeding 15p for every £1 staked.

Table 15: Handicap Chases Run in the Summer by Age of Runner

Age	Prop[n]	Wins	Runs	Wins%	Average Ret/£1
5yo	1%	6	75	8%	-£0.37
6yo	8%	46	269	17%	+£0.15
7yo	17%	96	605	16%	+£0.06
8yo	24%	135	904	15%	-£0.05
9yo	21%	114	1060	11%	-£0.30
10yo	14%	80	849	9%	-£0.19
11yo	6%	33	499	7%	-£0.45
12yo+	8%	43	517	8%	-£0.10

For all months, horses that were placed on their latest start took almost a third of all races, with previous race winners accounting for another 22% of wins. Over 50% of handicap chases were won by horses that had a recent success rate of between 10% and 25% based on their last ten races. Although over half of all handicap chases were won by horses priced at 4/1 or less, unlike handicap hurdle races odds on shots were not worth following.

Table 16: All Handicap Chases by Starting Price

Starting Price	Prop[n]	Wins	Runs	Wins%	Average Ret/£1
Odds On	3%	92	180	51%	-£0.11
Ev - 2/1	16%	463	1375	34%	-£0.12
9/4 - 4/1	31%	891	4323	21%	-£0.15
9/2 - 6/1	19%	550	3847	14%	-£0.11
13/2-10/1	18%	518	5290	10%	-£0.11
11/1-16/1	9%	258	4182	6%	-£0.11
18/1-33/1	3%	100	3409	3%	-£0.26
40/1+	0%	10	951	1%	-£0.46

A Selection of Flat Race Profiles

The following profiles apply to turf flat races and are very general in their form. Five complete seasons of data have been used (1999-2003) to generate the profiles which provide useful background data regarding the type of horse that can be expected to win the various race categories.

Two-Year-Old Races: Non-Handicaps

Two-year-old turf races are often dominated by unraced horses. However, even though all juveniles start their two-year-old season without any racing experience, only 22% of these races were won by unraced animals during the five years to end 2003.

In terms of time between races, over 50% of juvenile races were won by horses returning from a break of between 8 and 28 days. However, the average return remained constant for all periods of absence. With respect to starting price, over 60% of races were won by horses priced at 4/1 or less with odds on shots returning the smallest loss to backers.

Table 17: Juvenile Non-Handicaps by Course Absence

Days Since Last Run	Prop[n]	Wins	Runs	Wins%	Average Ret/£1
1..7	6%	215	1867	12%	-£0.36
8..14	23%	857	7161	12%	-£0.34
15..28	32%	1172	9538	12%	-£0.31
29..60	14%	516	4795	11%	-£0.35
61..100	3%	93	1062	9%	-£0.45
101+	1%	29	361	8%	-£0.28
Unraced	22%	835	12270	7%	-£0.43

Table 18: Juvenile Non-Handicaps by Starting Price

Starting Price	Prop[n]	Wins	Runs	Wins%	Average Ret/£1
Odds On	16%	612	993	62%	-£0.02
Ev - 2/1	21%	772	2068	37%	-£0.05
9/4 - 4/1	25%	931	4099	23%	-£0.08
9/2 - 6/1	13%	465	3313	14%	-£0.13
13/2-10/1	13%	475	5432	9%	-£0.20
11/1-16/1	7%	275	6118	4%	-£0.34
18/1-33/1	4%	165	9483	2%	-£0.55
40/1+	1%	22	5548	0%	-£0.78

Focussing on the juvenile Group races, it is interesting to note that the distribution of winners with respect to time between races changes. 87% of these races were won by horses running after an absence of between 8 and 60 days, with those returning from a break of between 8 and 14 days winning 20% of races and returning a profit of 6p for every £1 staked at starting price. Interestingly, the 41 horses running after a break of less than eight days all failed to win. One other significant feature of juvenile Group races is that 64% of races were won by horses that were successful on their latest run.

Table 19: Runners in Juvenile Group Races Analysed by Course Absence

Days Since Last Run	Propⁿ	Wins	Runs	Wins%	Average Ret/£1
1..7	0%	0	41	0%	-£1.00
8..14	20%	27	248	11%	+£0.06
15..28	32%	44	510	9%	-£0.35
29..60	33%	45	354	13%	-£0.21
61..100	5%	7	62	11%	-£0.45
101+	1%	2	23	9%	-£0.81

Maiden races often appear difficult to solve with many unraced horses to assess. However, it should be noted that the market tends to price these races very accurately with 60% of winners priced at 4/1 or less. Odds on shots produced the lowest average loss at starting price. Horses available at 11/1 or higher won only 13% of races with a success rate of just 2%. Consequently these horses returned a huge loss to starting price punters.

Table 20: Runners in Juvenile Maiden Races Analysed by Starting Price

Starting Price	Propⁿ	Wins	Runs	Wins%	Average Ret/£1
Odds On	17%	405	657	62%	-£0.02
Ev - 2/1	20%	477	1277	37%	-£0.06
9/4 - 4/1	24%	577	2464	23%	-£0.06
9/2 - 6/1	12%	284	2053	14%	-£0.14
13/2-10/1	13%	316	3536	9%	-£0.18
11/1-16/1	7%	174	4224	4%	-£0.39
18/1-33/1	5%	111	6958	1%	-£0.59
40/1+	1%	18	4181	0%	-£0.75

Two-Year-Old Races: Handicaps

Juvenile handicaps, or nursery races, start in July. Horses need to have raced three times or to have won at least one race before they are allocated a handicap mark and become eligible for these races. The handicap mark determines the amount of weight each horse carries and from Table 21 it can be seen that over the last five years 47% of nursery races were won by horses carrying between 9-0 and 9-07, these horses also returned the lowest loss to backers.

Table 21: Runners in Nursery Races Analysed by Weight Carried

Weight Carried	Prop[n]	Wins	Runs	Wins%	Average Ret/£1
9-8 ..10-00	1%	7	37	19%	-£0.50
9-0 .. 9-07	47%	289	2214	13%	-£0.12
8-8 .. 8-13	22%	133	1907	7%	-£0.36
8-0 .. 8-07	21%	132	1973	7%	-£0.33
..7-13	9%	53	1081	5%	-£0.32

Table 22: Runners in Nursery Races Analysed by Starting Price

Starting Price	Prop[n]	Wins	Runs	Wins%	Average Ret/£1
Odds On	2%	13	23	56%	-£0.02
Ev - 2/1	10%	63	154	41%	+£0.07
9/4 - 4/1	22%	136	682	20%	-£0.16
9/2 - 6/1	20%	124	840	14%	-£0.08
13/2-10/1	23%	144	1637	9%	-£0.19
11/1-16/1	16%	97	1930	5%	-£0.26
18/1-33/1	6%	36	1710	2%	-£0.47
40/1+	0%	1	233	0%	-£0.82

Table 23: Runners in Nursery Races Analysed by Run Number

Run Number	Propⁿ	Wins	Runs	Wins%	Average Ret/£1
3rd Run	9%	53	249	21%	+£0.16
4th Run	25%	154	1896	8%	-£0.30
5th Run	22%	136	1593	9%	-£0.29
6th+ Run	44%	271	3471	8%	-£0.28

With respect to starting price, horses priced between 13/2 and 10/1 won almost a quarter of races, though horses priced between evens and 2/1 returned a profit at starting price. Analysing the results by run number is also informative and from Table 23 it can be seen that apart from horses having their third run the results are uniformly distributed over the run number categories. However, horses that had run twice previously scored at a rate of one in five and returned a profit of 16p/£1.

Three-Year-Old Races: Claiming Races

Although horses in claiming races carry different weights, these are not set by the BHB Handicapper, but by the value placed on each animal. Over the last five seasons approximately 60% of claiming races were won by horses carrying between 8-00 and 8-13. However, in terms of profit the horses to follow are those allotted between 9-00 and 9-07. These horses won 31% of races and returned a profit at starting price of 3p/£1.

Table 24: Runners in 3-y.o Claiming Races Analysed by Weight Carried

Weight Carried	Propⁿ	Wins	Runs	Wins%	Average Ret/£1
9-8 ..10-00	1%	1	16	6%	-£0.88
9-0 .. 9-07	31%	54	261	21%	+£0.03
8-8 .. 8-13	29%	51	540	9%	-£0.27
8-0 .. 8-07	31%	55	863	6%	-£0.35
..7-13	9%	15	307	5%	-£0.18

Unlike other non-handicap races, only 46% of races were won by horses priced at 4/1 or less, but in a similar fashion, odds on shots proved most profitable.

Table 25: Runners in 3-y.o Claiming Races Analysed by Starting Price

Starting Price	Prop[n]	Wins	Runs	Wins%	Average Ret/£1
Odds On	5%	12	18	67%	+£0.16
Ev - 2/1	16%	29	87	33%	-£0.19
9/4 - 4/1	25%	44	212	21%	-£0.13
9/2 - 6/1	16%	29	195	15%	-£0.08
13/2-10/1	19%	33	312	11%	+£0.06
11/1-16/1	7%	12	357	3%	-£0.52
18/1-33/1	7%	13	534	2%	-£0.32
40/1+	2%	4	272	2%	-£0.29

Over a third of winners had raced within 8 and 14 days previously, and almost 70% had run unplaced on their latest start.

Three-Year-Old Races: Handicaps

There are many types of flat handicaps, including selling handicaps, Listed handicaps and maiden handicaps. The following profiles exclude these special classifications and focus on standard handicap races open to three-year-olds only.

In terms of starting price, the winners of three-year-old handicaps over the last five years were spread quite uniformly over the price bands. However, with respect to average return to the bettor, the degree of underpricing appears to increase significantly for horses starting at 13/2 or higher. This is illustrated by Table 26, where it can be seen that the average loss is approximately 9p/£1 for horses starting at 6/1 or less then increases to 22p and higher for the longer priced runners.

Table 26: Runners in 3-y.o Handicap Races Analysed by Starting Price

Starting Price	Prop[n]	Wins	Runs	Wins%	Average Ret/£1
Odds On	2%	50	106	47%	-£0.20
Ev - 2/1	10%	203	609	33%	-£0.13
9/4 - 4/1	24%	484	2259	21%	-£0.10
9/2 - 6/1	19%	378	2530	15%	-£0.07
13/2-10/1	23%	473	5309	9%	-£0.18
11/1-16/1	14%	284	6216	5%	-£0.34
18/1-33/1	7%	152	6600	2%	-£0.42
40/1+	0%	9	1172	1%	-£0.61

During the five seasons, 63% of winners had raced between 8 and 28 days previously with horses off the track for 60 days or more taking just 9% of races a returning a massive loss at starting price. Though 27% of winners had been placed on their latest run, 51% had been unplaced.

Table 27: Runners in 3-y.o Handicap Races Analysed by Course Absence

Days Since Last Run	Prop[n]	Wins	Runs	Wins%	Average Ret/£1
1..7	14%	277	2486	11%	-£0.19
8..14	27%	555	6392	9%	-£0.30
15..28	36%	728	8444	9%	-£0.23
29..60	14%	285	3785	8%	-£0.28
61..100	2%	38	804	5%	-£0.45
101+	7%	150	2857	5%	-£0.43

Table 28: Runners in 3-y.o Handicap Races Analysed by Weight Carried

Weight Carried	Prop[n]	Wins	Runs	Wins%	Average Ret/£1
10-01+	0%	5	57	9%	-£0.33
9-8 ..10-00	2%	32	97	33%	+£0.03
9-0 .. 9-07	46%	927	8871	10%	-£0.24
8-8 .. 8-13	26%	519	6405	8%	-£0.30
8-0 .. 8-07	19%	394	6084	6%	-£0.31
..7-13	8%	156	3287	5%	-£0.32

Weight carried is always an interesting feature of this particular race classification. And from Table 28 it can be seen that horses carrying between 9-00 and 9-07 won the largest share of races. Interestingly this profile only changes slightly when the ground turns soft or heavy, with the categories covering the range 8-08 to 9-07 still accounting for approximately 70% of all race winners. On fast going (i.e. good to firm or firmer) horses in the 9-0 to 9-07 range won 47% of races but those set to carry between 9-08 and 10-00 returned the best profit at starting price (19p/£1).

Table 29: Runners in 3-y.o Handicap Races Run on Soft or Heavy Going Analysed by Weight Carried

Weight Carried	Prop[n]	Wins	Runs	Wins%	Average Ret/£1
9-8 ..10-00	0%	0	9	0%	-£1.00
9-0 .. 9-07	44%	87	902	10%	-£0.29
8-8 .. 8-13	31%	61	667	9%	-£0.23
8-0 .. 8-07	15%	30	642	5%	-£0.46
..7-13	10%	20	356	6%	-£0.15

Table 30: Runners in 3-y.o Handicap Races Run Good to Firm or Faster Going Analysed by Weight Carried

Weight Carried	Prop[n]	Wins	Runs	Wins%	Average Ret/£1
10-01+	0%	3	33	9%	-£0.24
9-8 ..10-00	2%	20	51	39%	+£0.19
9-0 .. 9-07	47%	522	4669	11%	-£0.22
8-8 .. 8-13	25%	276	3333	8%	-£0.29
8-0 .. 8-07	19%	209	3046	7%	-£0.32
..7-13	7%	82	1714	5%	-£0.35

All Age Races: Group Races

In general All-Age races are open to all non-juveniles. There will be a few exceptions, such as races for four-year-olds only and on occasion two-year-olds are allowed to compete.

Four-year-olds have won the largest proportion of All-Age Group races during the last five years. And between them, three and four-year-olds took almost two-thirds of these events. However, five-year-olds returned the lowest loss to bettors. Horses rated between 110 and 119 by the BHB won 50% of races, though horses rated over 119 returned the best profit at starting price.

Table 31: Runners in All-Age Group Races Analysed by Age

Age	Prop^n	Wins	Runs	Wins%	Average Ret/£1
3yo	28%	87	796	11%	-£0.36
4yo	33%	104	998	10%	-£0.20
5yo	23%	72	520	14%	-£0.03
6yo	8%	25	291	9%	-£0.40
7yo	4%	14	140	10%	-£0.25
8yo	3%	7	83	8%	-£0.27
9yo	0%	1	33	3%	-£0.83
10yo	1%	4	18	22%	+£0.33

Table 32: Runners in All-Age Group Races Analysed by BHB Rating

BHB Rating	Prop^n	Wins	Runs	Wins%	Average Ret/£1
120..139	12%	38	149	26%	+£0.10
110..119	50%	157	1207	13%	-£0.21
100..109	19%	60	906	7%	-£0.38
90 .. 99	3%	9	173	5%	-£0.45
70 .. 89	0%	1	53	2%	-£0.72
50 .. 69	0%	0	3	0%	-£1.00
Unrated	16%	49	388	13%	-£0.01

All Age Races: Maiden Races

Older horses should be avoided in all-age maiden races. Over the last five seasons 87% of these races were won by three-year-olds with runners aged five and older winning just 15 races (2%). With respect to ratings, 50% of the winners were unrated; however, horses rated 90 or higher by the BHB did return a small profit at starting price. Over 70% of winners were priced at 4/1 or less with horses starting at 11/1 or longer taking just 8% of races. Those priced between evens and 2/1 returned the lowest deficit to backers.

Table 33: Runners in All-Age Maiden Races Analysed by Age

Age	Prop^n	Wins	Runs	Wins%	Average Ret/£1
3yo	87%	755	5994	13%	-£0.37
4yo	11%	96	1747	6%	-£0.62
5yo	1%	10	485	2%	-£0.87
6yo	0%	4	142	3%	-£0.66
7yo	0%	1	78	1%	-£1.00
8yo	0%	0	25	0%	-£1.00
9yo	0%	0	21	0%	-£1.00
10yo	0%	0	4	0%	-£1.00
11yo+	0%	0	12	0%	-£1.00

Table 34: Runners in All-Age Maiden Races Analysed by BHB Rating

BHB Rating	Prop^n	Wins	Runs	Wins%	Average Ret/£1
110..119	0%	2	2	100%	+£0.68
100..109	1%	6	18	33%	-£0.49
90 .. 99	3%	30	52	58%	+£0.23
70 .. 89	33%	285	1073	27%	-£0.11
50 .. 69	10%	84	896	9%	-£0.28
..49	3%	24	1151	2%	-£0.62
Unrated	50%	435	5295	8%	-£0.54

All Age Races: Handicaps

Age appears to be an important factor in these handicap races. Over the last five years 56% of these races were won by horses aged four or five. 79% of winners had raced within 28 days, with horses returning from an absence of 61 days or more taking just 10% of races. Interestingly, only 17% of races were won by horses that had won their previous race, with 57% of races going to horses unplaced on their latest start.

Table 35: Runners in All-Age Handicap Races Analysed by Age

Age	Prop^n	Wins	Runs	Wins%	Average Ret/£1
3yo	15%	858	12126	7%	-£0.40
4yo	32%	1826	26109	7%	-£0.29
5yo	24%	1331	15836	8%	-£0.19
6yo	14%	796	10234	8%	-£0.24
7yo	7%	424	6122	7%	-£0.31
8yo	4%	230	3734	6%	-£0.39
9yo	2%	118	1957	6%	-£0.32
10yo	1%	50	992	5%	-£0.52
11yo+	0%	27	542	5%	-£0.37

Conclusions

Race profiling can provide valuable information for the bettor whether it is to support his/her selection or otherwise. In the previous section a few profiles associated with the main race types are presented. However, to get the best from this approach it is necessary to use specifically designed computer software which allows the user to enter various race characteristics in order to generate the most relevant profile. Such software is easily constructed and can be developed with any database facility, alternatively existing inexpensive packages can be downloaded over the internet from www.pjmracing.com.

CHAPTER 2
THE EFFECT OF WEIGHT IN FLAT HANDICAPS

The effect of weight on the speed at which a horse can run has been widely debated. There appears to be two opposing camps: those who believe that the more weight a horse carries the slower it will run, and those who feel sure that a weight increase makes no material difference. So is there any way of deciding whether weight does have an effect and if it does can a relationship between weight and effect be determined so that it can be accurately reflected in the handicapping process?

The Evidence for a Weight Effect

For Flat race handicaps it is generally accepted that the horses higher in the weights are the more likely winners. It is easy to support this view by analysing historical results and generating a simple table showing success rate by weight carried. From this we can immediately see that those horses at the top of the handicap tend to have a better strike rate than those receiving weight. In fact, over five seasons horses set to carry 9-08 or more recorded a success rate of 9.5%, whereas those carrying between 8-01 and 8-07 won at a frequency of just 5.4% (see Table 1). Now this says little about the effect of weight, though it could be concluded that simply by increasing the weight a horse has to carry does not seem to impair its chance of success since the higher weights win more often.

However, when this success rate is subdivided by the going a more interesting pattern is found. On fast going (i.e. ground officially recorded as good to firm, firm or hard) the highest weighted horses recorded a success rate of just over 10%, yet on soft going this figure reduced to just 7.3%. There must be a reason for this change, and the obvious assumption is that the weight is having a greater effect when the ground is soft than when it rides fast. Logically this is a sound assumption and the data support this further with a success rate of 8.4% (a figure between the high and low values) for ground classified in the mid range categories of good and good to soft.

Table 1: Analysis of Success Rate (%) by Weight Carried and Going
Non-Juvenile Handicaps 1998-2002

Weight Carried	Fast	Gd/GS	Soft	AW	All
9-08 - 10-00	10.2	8.4	7.3	10.7	9.5
9-01 - 9-07	9.4	8.1	7.5	10.3	9.0
8-08 - 9-00	7.7	7.2	8.0	8.3	7.7
8-01 - 8-07	6.9	6.4	6.2	7.5	6.7
7-08 - 8-00	5.3	4.8	5.2	6.8	5.4
Total	7.9	7.1	7.1	8.8	7.7

Based on the evidence presented in Table 1 it is difficult to conclude that weight is not having an effect. Also this is the more logical conclusion. After all if weight has no effect then there is no limit to the amount of weight a horse can carry without racing any slower. Consequently a horse should run as well carrying 300 pounds as it does carrying 126 pounds, which is clearly nonsense. Whilst slight additions to the amount of weight carried may not make any measurable effect, as the weight increases its effect will become apparent, though it needs to be established at what point the effect becomes measurable.

So assuming that weight does have an effect, why do the top-weights win more often on fast ground as well as on All Weather tracks? One reason for this is the weight scale used to convert the distance a horse is beaten into an equivalent weight figure in pounds for future adjustments to handicap ratings. Since handicaps are framed for all horses on all types of ground, then it is reasonable to expect these adjustments to work best on an "average" surface, such as good ground, and for the method to over-compensate and under-compensate for horses running on going either side of this mid category. The further the ground differs from the mid point the greater the effect, either to the advantage of the top weights or to their disadvantage. Table 1 appears to support this hypothesis, which implies the weight scale is either incorrect or needs expanding to cover the differences in surfaces as well as race distances.

Weight Handicapping Based on Form

Once qualified for a handicap race, a horse is assigned a handicap mark by the BHB handicappers. The aim of this artificial handicapping is to give all horses the same chance of winning races by penalising the better animals by giving them more weight to carry. This mark is equivalent to a form rating and is a convenient way of expressing the ability of one horse relative to another. Handicap marks are expressed in pounds, therefore if two three-year-old colts were rated 104 and 108, the latter could be said to be 4 pounds superior to the former, and in a handicap race would carry 4 pounds more weight.

Handicap ratings are adjusted after each race, with the mark of the winner increased on most occasions, and those of horses thought to be too high in the handicap, based on the race performance, reduced. In order to assess whether a horse has run to its current handicap mark the race is examined in detail and normally a benchmark horse is determined. This horse is deemed to have run to a specific mark and is normally a well exposed, consistent runner. The other horses are then assessed with respect to this runner. The basis of the handicap adjustments is the distance, in horse lengths, between the horses at the finish of a race, converted to pounds (weight) using a scale based on the race distance. This weight scale can be approximated by the following formula:

pounds (weight) = distance beaten in lengths x 15
                    race distance (f)

Thus if horse A beats horse B by 2 lengths in a 5 furlong race (both carrying the same weight) the superiority in pounds would be estimated at approximately 6lbs (i.e. 2 x 15 / 5). For an equivalent distance between the horses in a 12 furlong race the superiority would be 2½lbs. This conversion is given in tabular form in Table 2.

Table 2: Distance to Weight Approximation

Race distance (f)	5f	6f	7f	8f	10f	12f	14f
pounds per length	3	2.5	2.1	1.9	1.5	1.2	1.1

This conversion provides a basis for calculating the weight adjustments, but the final weight rise/reduction is determined by the handicapper and can vary substantially from race to race depending on the handicapper's assessment of the differences in ability between the runners. For example, although a horse may win by only 1 length, the manner of the victory may result in the handicapper basing its future rating on a win equivalent to, say, 4 lengths. This can give rise to disagreements between the handicappers and the trainers who feel their horses have been harshly treated.

So not only does weight handicapping depend on the assessment of the correct bench-mark horses it also crucially depends on this weight per distance scale.

Generating a New Weight Scale for All Weather Racing

In order to use a statistical approach to approximate the weight scale it is necessary to examine a large sample of historical races. For this example all seven-furlong races run on Lingfield's All Weather track constitute the sample. In order to reduce the noise in the data the sample is further restricted to the winners of non-juvenile handicap races. It is characterised by the following features:

Average (mean) race time of the winner: 86.7 seconds

Average (mean) BHB rating of the winner: 63

Average (mean) weight carried by the winner: 126 lbs (9-00)

From the sample it is a straightforward task to determine that the higher (BHB) rated runners take, on average, less time to run the seven furlongs. This is to be expected since they are the better animals. Once the data have been normalised for weight carried, a regression method can be used to generate the time reduction. For the seven-furlong course at Lingfield this factor is approximately 0.0485 seconds per 1lb in weight or 1 point on the BHB handicap scale. In other words a horse rated 80 will run the course 0.0485 seconds faster than one carrying the same weight and rated 79, on average.

Since 1 point on the BHB rating scale equates to 1lb in weight carried (i.e. if a horse is rated 1 point higher than another it will carry one pound more in a handicap) then a relationship can be determined between weight and race time as follows:

7 furlongs = 1540 yards

assuming one horse length = 3 yards, then 7 furlongs = 513.3 lengths

average race time (7f) = 86.7 seconds,

therefore the horses run at 5.92 lengths per second (5.92 = 513.3/86.7)

from the historical results we know that 1lb = 0.0485s,

so 1 second = 20.62 lbs,

and therefore 1 length = 20.62/5.92 = 3.5lbs

Consequently to slow the horse by one length requires an extra 3.5lbs of weight over a distance of seven furlongs at Lingfield. Using the existing weight scale the figure would be nearer 2.1lbs. So there exists a significant difference between the scale currently used and one which would be based on the above calculation.

A New All Weather Weight Scale

The above method can be used to generate a weight scale for any track and any race distance. However, having a different scale for each distance at each track would be difficult to use when manually handicapping horses, though for computer-based handicapping this is an option. To simplify the weight scale it is necessary to generate a single scale similar to the one given in Table 2, which is applicable to all three All Weather tracks.

The process used to generate a single weight scale is similar to the one detailed above with the additional adjustments for track speed and the ability of the runners. The conventional approach to making the adjustment is to use standard, or median, race times to normalise for the differences in track speed. However, more sophisticated methods using artificial neural networks are now often used which avoid the possibility of introducing additional errors in the form of erroneous standard times. Adjustments are also required for the difference between the average ability levels for the horses running at the different tracks (though for the All Weather this is of only minimal significance). This is a simple procedure since all horses have a BHB handicap rating, so their merits can be easily compared and a suitable normalising factor determined.

After normalisation and smoothing to reduce the noise, the following weight scale can be generated for All Weather races:

Table 3: Distance to Weight Approximation for All Weather Racing

Race distance (f)	5f	6f	7f	8f	10f	12f	14f
pounds per length	4.8	4.0	3.4	3.0	2.4	2.0	1.7

There are two main differences between this scale and the one presented in Table 2. The first is the magnitude of the figures. Under the new scale horses racing over five furlongs could expect their penalties to increase by an additional 1.8lbs per length. The second difference relates to the form of the scale. The original scale is linear, this one is clearly non-linear which can be seen from Graph 1 which presents the scale of weight per length beaten.

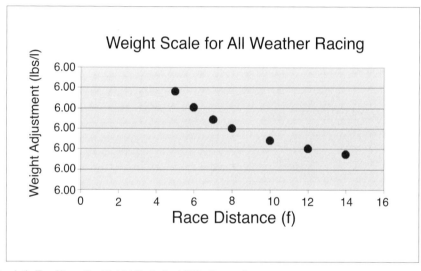

Graph 1: The Alternative Weight Scale for All Weather racing

Conclusions

Based on the data presented in Table 1, weight does have an effect on the outcome of horse-races by increasing the average time it takes for a horse to run a specified distance. However, whilst the current approach to weight handicapping is producing competitive racing there appears to be conditions under which the weight scale is not as effective. This is to be expected when any general linear normalising or approximation approach is applied to a non-linear domain. Though on average it is the best model, such a technique will not provide the best approximation for areas of the domain where the conditions differ markedly from the norm. In the weight scale case this appears to be when the ground approaches the extremes. Consequently it is possible for bettors to benefit by developing more specific methods that can account for the variations in the domain.

The method outlined in this article used All Weather racing as the case study. However, it can be applied to any type of racing, and extended to cover different ground conditions and track formations. For instance it may be found to be beneficial to have two weight scales for mile races: one for races run on straight courses and another for round course races. Using a range of weight scales will only improve the quality of ratings which could provide the private handicapper with a significant advantage, though it does complicate the handicapping process.

CHAPTER 3:
ASSESSING AND EXPLOITING THE EFFECT OF THE DRAW

In recent years the draw has become a very popular talking point with race commentators. Which side of the track will be favoured, has the watering negated the traditional draw bias, and does the inside running rail provide an advantage to the low drawn runners? Such questions are posed and discussed before, during and after almost every flat race, which has pushed the draw to the forefront of race analysis.

During the early 1990s I followed the draw very closely during the turf season, and systems based on this critical factor made up at least 80% of my Summer betting. At the time Ripon was by far the best "draw track" in the country especially the six furlong course. Stalls 1 and 2 in non-juvenile handicaps were the ones to follow and from 1991 to 1996 there were 127 runners from these two stalls producing 25 winners and returning profit of £83.10 to a level £1 stake at starting price. In very large fields (18 or more runners) a strategy of combining the lowest two stalls with the highest two also worked well, producing good tricast and dual forecast returns on several occasions. Nowadays this bias seems to have disappeared, but there are other tracks which offer draw followers plenty of betting opportunities.

Determining the Draw Bias

There are two approaches that can be used to assess the effect of the draw. The first is based on the expected number of winners from each stall and is ideally suited to the system follower; the second method uses finishing distances to determine a measure of the bias by stall and is essential to those who build computer models with ability ratings (form or speed) as an input. The following sections provide the details behind these two methods.

The aim of a racing system is to identify a rule or method that will return a profit over a period of time. One approach to developing draw-based systems is to determine the profitable stalls to follow. To achieve this it is necessary to anaylse a sample of races for every race distance at each track.

Handicap races are chosen in preference to non-handicaps since the ability range of the runners is normalised by the allocation of different weights by the BHB handicappers, therefore only a small external effect (such as the draw) will make a noticeable change to the result of the race. In non-handicaps the ability range is likely to be much wider, and even with the best draw of the race and a ten lengths start a large proportion of the runners would still fail to win. In other words, the draw will not, in most cases, be a significant determining factor in non-handicaps, the crucial element being the ability of the horses. A similar argument can be applied to nurseries, although not to quite the same extent. Unexposed two-year-old horses are exceptionally difficult to handicap and therefore their varying levels of ability will not be accounted for as well as it is for older horses.

To calculate whether horses drawn in a specific stall have an advantage, it is necessary to compute three figures: the number of winners from each stall, the expected number of winners from each stall and the level stake return. The first figure is easily determined, similarly the profit/loss figure, but the expected number of winners needs further explanation. Since the draw is made randomly one method for calculating this figure is to take the reciprocal of the number of runners in each race and aggregate these fractions. So, as an example, in a ten runner race each stall would have an expectation of 1/10 and in a 20 runner race this figure would reduce to 1/20. The combined expectation for the stalls 1-10 based on the two races is 1/10 + 1/20, or 3/20. It should be noted that for each race the sum of the expectation figures must equal one, the number of actual winners per race.

As an example the figures given in Table 1 were derived for the five furlong course at Brighton based on the five years 1998-2002:

Table 1: Number of winners compared to the expected number of winners for the Brighton 5 Furlong track

Stall Number	Number of Winners	Expected No. of Winners	Profit/Loss to £1 Stake
1	2	3.7	-£26.00
2	7	3.7	-£2.09
3	4	3.7	+£4.25
4	6	3.7	+£7.75

From Table 1 it can be seen that stall 2 produced seven winners in non-juvenile handicap races during the period of analysis compared to an expected number of just 3.7. Whilst this is an impressive statistic, it is not supported by the stalls 1 and 3 and with a negative return it would not provide the basis for a system without introducing other factors. The figures given in Table 2, though, are far more appealing from a betting angle.

Table 2: Number of winners compared to the expected number of winners for the Epsom 8½ Furlong track

Stall Number	Number of Winners	Expected No. of Winners	Profit/Loss to £1 Stake
1	2	2.5	-£9.00
2	3	2.5	+£3.00
3	3	2.5	+£20.50
4	4	2.5	+£32.50

For the 28 races analysed it can be seen that the track possesses a bias towards the low drawn runners, and that this bias would have been extremely profitable over the five seasons of the analysis period. Though the number of winners is higher than the expected number I tend to prefer this figure to be at least twice the expectation so further analysis would be required before betting.

In order to determine whether the high draw horses have an advantage it is necessary to calculate the same figures but as opposed to starting from stall 1, it is necessary to consider each stall in relation to the highest drawn horse in the race. Therefore, in a twenty-runner race, stall twenty becomes stall zero and stall nineteen becomes stall one for analysis purposes. And in an eight-runner race, stall eight becomes stall zero and stall seven becomes stall one etc. The analysis can then be performed as for the low draw method.

The main criticism of this approach concerns the use of the reciprocal of the number of runners to derive the expected number of winners. However, this is easily justified because the large sample size and random allocation of draw will result in the winners, on unbiased tracks, being uniformly distributed across the stalls without favour to any particular position. Consequently using a constant in this respect is valid. However, it is important not to use variables such as starting price to set the expectation. Though starting price is representative of the chance of success it accounts for the draw and hence is a biased measure.

This type of analysis indicates quite clearly the tracks with potentially profitable biases. However, further investigation of the likely candidates is required before parting with any money. Draw biases appear and disappear over time. Ten years ago there were many more biases than there are now. This reduction in the number of biased tracks is mainly due to changes to the courses themselves and the watering policies. So any analysis needs to account for possible changes over time. Table 3 illustrates the profit/loss breakdown for the Epsom 8½ furlong track by season.

Table 3: Year-By-Year Draw Analysis for Epsom 8½ Furlong track

Stalls 1-4	1998	1999	2000	2001	2002	All Years
Winners	1	2	3	5	1	12
Runners	20	24	22	24	20	110
Profit to £1	-£10.00	-£6.50	+£26.00	+£49.50	-£12.00	+£47.00

As Table 3 illustrates there would have been three losing years following the draw at Epsom, but overall the profit is reasonable. The bias still appears to have an effect though the poor performance in the final year of analysis is worrying. Under these circumstances further checking would be required before adding this track to the courses to follow since there may have been changes made to the course at the end of the 2001 season which removed the bias. For Epsom, though, this is unlikely because the draw bias is a direct result of the configuration of the track. On a straight course changes made to the drainage could significantly affect the bias, and had these statistics been derived from a straight course they would need to be viewed with extreme caution.

Such systems are prone to long losing runs as the percentage success rate of just over 15% for Epsom implies, so if you require a high volume of winners this may not be the best system to follow. Naturally more detailed analyses can be performed, dividing the historical races by going and stall placement is also informative. However, it is important to note that this will reduce the number of races for analysis so more care is required with the follow-up work and comparisons with the expected number of winners.

The tracks listed have been identified as having a significant draw bias using data collected from the five years 1999-2003, and these trends may continue in the future.

Improving the Success Rate by Considering Running Styles

The main problem with systems based on the draw is the success rate. Such methods generally produce one winner every five bets, and this low strike rate means that long losing runs are inevitable. Fortunately it is possible to improve the strike rate by considering other factors, such as the price the horse started for its last race, the current price, and running styles. In handicap races, the type in which the draw produces the best return, there is a strong correlation between the success rate and the starting price of the horse for its latest race. The longer the price the less likely the horse is to win. So in order to increase the success rate of the system, selections which started at long prices for their last race, such as 33/1 or higher, can be omitted. Naturally this will lead to missing good priced winners, so as an alternative the stake on these horses can be reduced.

Another key element is the number of runners in the race. In very small fields, the effect of the bias will not be so crucial. For instance, in a four-runner 5 furlong sprint at Haydock with the stalls on the stands' side, all the runners could be considered to be benefiting from the draw, with the poorest drawn horse (in stall 1) being only a few yards from the favoured running rail. For draw followers the larger the field the better, since an increasingly greater proportion of the runners will be suffering from a poor draw yet their presence in the race will help to inflate the price of the better drawn runners. From an analysis of the data, it has been found only races with seven or more runners should be considered for betting purposes.

One further consideration for betting on the draw is the running style of the selection. It is important in sprints and races which are run on the turn in the first few furlongs to select horses with good early pace. A slow starting animal can lose a good position within a matter of strides and then have to round part or all of the field to have any chance of winning, completely negating the positive effect of the draw. Naturally, it is difficult to tell whether the selection has a good early pace. In the absence of sectional timing, the next best guide is the comment-in-running associated with the animal's recent runs. The key words to check for include: held up, started slowly, missed break, always behind, outpaced early. It is good policy to avoid horses which have received these, or similar, comments on recent runs.

Another issue concerning the style of running that can impact on the result of a draw-based system is the ability of the jockey to get a good start. Some jockeys seem more adept at getting their horses out of the stalls quickly, and these are worth following. Table 4 lists the performances of a selection of jockeys in 5-6 furlong races through the 2001 and 2002 turf seasons. On average a horse either dwelt at the start, started slowly or missed the break 7% of the time. Clearly, from Table 4 it can be seen that some jockeys appear capable of reducing the proportion to very low levels.

Track	Stalls Position	Draw Bias
Beverley 5F	Any	High numbers have a considerable advantage with 23 winners recorded from the highest three stalls in recent years, three times the expectation.
Beverley 8F	Any	High numbers have the advantage – the top six stalls have won almost 80% of non-juvenile handicap races in recent seasons.
Chepstow 8F	Any	Horses drawn high seem to have an advantage with the highest two stalls producing 12 winners significantly higher than the expectation and also returning a huge profit at starting price.
Chester 12F	Any	The tight track favours those drawn low. However this is well-known and profits have disappeared for the sprint races. Over 1m4f the bias remains and does not appear to have been fully accounted for in the starting price.
Doncaster 7F	Any	Runners drawn in the highest five stalls have won over half of the non-juvenile handicaps over the last five years, returning a profit of over 50p/£1 at starting price.
Goodwood 7F	Any	A looping right-handed track favours the highest drawn runners. Over five years the top two stalls have won at a rate exceeding twice the expectation and have returned a healthy profit.
Salisbury 12-14F	Any	The highest stall has been worth following in recent seasons producing 17 winners from 69 runners.
Windsor 5F	Any	Top three stalls have won half of the non-juvenile handicaps run since 1999 and have returned a good profit at starting price.
York 7½F	Any	The lowest three stalls have been worth following in recent years returning a profit of over 80p/£1 at starting price.
Hamilton 8F	High numbers against the rail	With stalls against the inside running-rail, the advantage is gained by the high numbers. The top six stalls have produced the vast majority of winners, though the profit is not exceptional.
Kempton 7F Jubilee	High numbers against the rail	The configuration of the track favours high-drawn horses which has resulted in nine winners from the top two stalls and a reasonable profit.
Ripon 12F	High numbers against the rail	The round track favours the high-drawn horses, but for the best profits bets should be kept to 12F races. The highest five stalls have produced 30 of the 35 latest winners.
Epsom 8½F	Low numbers against the rail	The round left-handed course gives the low numbers the advantage. Over five years the bias has produced 14 winners from 116 runners from the lowest four stalls, with horses drawn three and four returning excellent profits.
Warwick 6F-12F	Low numbers against the rail	This oval-shaped track favours the low drawn runners and over the last five years these have been worth following.

Table 4: Proportion of slow starts in sprint races by jockey

Jockey	Rides	Slow Starts	% Slow Starts
S. Whitworth	118	17	14.4%
P. Fessey	76	10	13.2%
D. Kinsella	132	17	12.9%
R. Brisland	56	7	12.5%
F. P. Ferris	66	8	12.1%
P. M. Quinn	83	10	12.0%
J. Quinn	101	12	11.9%
P. Hanagan	179	21	11.7%
G. Bardwell	62	7	11.3%
D. Nolan	54	6	11.1%
T. G. McLaughlin	64	7	10.9%
G. Sparkes	65	7	10.8%
M. Savage	96	10	10.4%
J. Mackay	136	14	10.3%
S. Sanders	179	18	10.1%
Dean McKeown	120	12	10.0%
J. P. Spencer	101	10	9.9%
J. Bramhill	128	12	9.4%
C. Rutter	88	8	9.1%
Darren Williams	114	10	8.8%
J. McAuley	93	8	8.6%
Joanna Badger	140	12	8.6%
R. Winston	199	17	8.5%
Dane O'Neill	107	9	8.4%
T. E. Durcan	122	10	8.2%
L. P. Keniry	98	8	8.2%
Paul Eddery	88	7	8.0%
Kim Tinkler	126	10	7.9%
Pat Eddery	143	11	7.7%
T. Hamilton	78	6	7.7%
I. Mongan	118	9	7.6%
Clare Roche	68	5	7.4%
E. Ahern	68	5	7.4%
M. Fenton	137	10	7.3%
M. Tebbutt	70	5	7.1%
B. Doyle	56	4	7.1%
N. Callan	100	7	7.0%
Alex Greaves	131	9	6.9%
A. Clark	74	5	6.8%
S. Carson	136	9	6.6%
D. Corby	91	6	6.6%
F. Lynch	198	13	6.6%
R.Hughes	130	8	6.2%
Martin Dwyer	115	7	6.1%
K. Fallon	181	11	6.1%

Table 4: continued

Jockey	Rides	Slow Starts	% Slow Starts
J. Carroll	150	9	6.0%
G. Duffield	170	10	5.9%
T. Williams	154	9	5.8%
G. Baker	103	6	5.8%
D. Sweeney	107	6	5.6%
Dale Gibson	166	9	5.4%
A. Beech	56	3	5.4%
F. Norton	189	10	5.3%
S. Drowne	171	9	5.3%
L. Newman	57	3	5.3%
K. Dalgleish	173	9	5.2%
T. Quinn	138	7	5.1%
M. Henry	80	4	5.0%
K. Darley	202	10	5.0%
D. R. McCabe	61	3	4.9%
G. Carter	61	3	4.9%
L. Dettori	61	3	4.9%
P. Doe	103	5	4.9%
N. Pollard	63	3	4.8%
W. Supple	172	8	4.7%
O. Pears	87	4	4.6%
R. Mullen	89	4	4.5%
J. Fanning	166	7	4.2%
S. Hitchcott	121	5	4.1%
P. Fitzsimons	225	9	4.0%
A. Culhane	127	5	3.9%
D. Holland	155	6	3.9%
D. Mernagh	141	5	3.5%
D. Allan	85	3	3.5%
P. Robinson	85	3	3.5%
C. Catlin	228	8	3.5%
J. Fortune	114	4	3.5%
G. Gibbons	91	3	3.3%
P. Dobbs	65	2	3.1%
T. Lucas	65	2	3.1%
P. Bradley	80	2	2.5%
A. Nicholls	191	4	2.1%
G. Hind	50	1	2.0%
R. Ffrench	52	1	1.9%
L. Enstone	54	1	1.9%
J. Tate	66	1	1.5%
J. Edmunds	63	0	0.0%
M. Hills	50	0	0.0%

Michael Hills and Jason Edmunds have exceptional ability at starting well, since neither had a poor start throughout the two seasons.

Quantifying the Draw Bias

Whilst an analysis of the success rates of horses running from each stall indicates whether high or low numbers are favoured on a particular track, this will not provide an explicit numerical value of the advantage afforded to each runner. In order to determine the effect in terms of distance advantage it is necessary to consider the distance between the horses at the finish of each race by stall number. However, simply analysing the average distance each horse is beaten by the race winner on a stall-by-stall basis would yield biased results. Since the allocation of stall numbers always starts from one, in small fields the winner must be drawn low; and in large fields for the horses drawn high to win they must beat more opponents. To overcome this bias it is necessary to relate the analysis to a specific stall (the "base stall") and calculate the advantage/disadvantage relative to this draw position. The best policy is to select the stall closest to the rail as the base stall then calculate the average distances relative to it. On left-handed tracks, when the stalls are placed against the inner rail the base stall is stall one. On a right-handed track with stalls against in inside rail the base stall becomes the highest in the race. On this basis the average distance beaten for all horses in the base stall will be zero. A negative average figure for other stalls implies they are disadvantaged by the draw relative to the base stall. A positive value indicates a draw advantage compared to the base stall. The graph illustrates the average distance the runners in 8½ furlong races at Epsom finished in relation to the horse running from stall one. Again only non-juvenile handicap races have been used for the reasons stated previously.

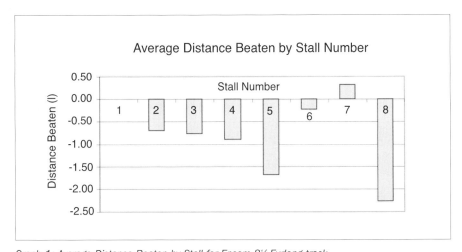

Graph 1: Average Distance Beaten by Stall for Epsom 8½ Furlong track

From the graph it can be seen that, on average, the horses drawn high are at a disadvantage compared to the stall one runner. For instance, the horses in stall eight are beaten, on average, about 2¼ lengths by the horses running from stall one for the races analysed.

This is not surprising since the 8½ furlong course at Epsom is run around a tight bend, and consequently the horses drawn wide have further to race than those drawn on the inside. Fitting a trend line to these data indicates that the disadvantage to horses drawn in stalls other than stall one is equivalent to 0.2 lengths per stall. In other words a horse drawn in stall five has a disadvantage of approximately 1 length (i.e. 0.2x5) to overcome.

Naturally before using these data in a forecasting model it is necessary to check for other influences, for instance the going effect. The easiest way to do this is to apply the model to a data set and analyse by the factor that is thought to affect the outcome. A distinct pattern to the results implies that the variable has an influence on the result and should be included in the model. A variable with no effect will exhibit a random pattern. As an example consider the follow table of residuals:

Table 5: Example of Residuals

Going Category	Residual
Good to firm	0.4
Good	0.0
Good to soft	-0.5
Soft	-1.5
Heavy	-2.5

From the data presented in Table 5 it is clear that the residuals are increasing as the ground softens and it can be concluded that the going has an effect on the bias. Consequently the factor relating to the ground conditions would need to be included in the analysis. Once the modelling has been completed the values can be converted from lengths to pounds using an appropriate and applied directly to the ratings in the forecasting model.

Summary

The draw remains the most interesting feature of Flat handicap races, without it these races would make no appeal whatsoever from a betting perspective. Whilst there are fewer tracks with draw biases than 10 years ago, opportunities remain for punters to exploit this feature and make a profit providing the data is analysed and validated with care.

CHAPTER 4
ESTIMATING STAMINA AND ABILITY FROM PEDIGREES

Often the racing press will report in its race analysis section that based on pedigree a particular horse will be suited by a certain race distance, or that another runner will appreciate racing over further or on a softer surface. Race commentators refer to the same statistics in their pre-race discussion. But how can these assessments be made accurately, and is there any numerical justification for them?

Such assessments are made purely from the animal's pedigree. Like humans, horses pass traits to their off-spring. These traits may be with respect to appearance, temperament, or more importantly for the racing enthusiast, ability and preferences for specific racing conditions such as the distance and ground conditions. For instance, the offspring of some sires will not be seen to their best until they get to race over middle distances, and the progeny of others will only produce their best on soft going. In many cases these preferences mirror those of their parents.

Consequently it should be possible to estimate such factors as speed and stamina from an examination of the animal's pedigree. This type of information could prove useful to bettors hoping to gain an edge in races where the runners are inexperienced and unexposed, and especially in ante post betting for the Classics.

Dosage

Since the early 1980s American Handicappers have used a method termed "Dosage" to classify pedigree types. The current version of the Dosage method is generally accredited to Dr S Roman, but its origins can be traced back to the work of Lt. Col. J. J. Vuillier and Franco Varola in the early part of the twentieth century. Roman was able to combine the work of these two pedigree experts to generate a more usable form of the Dosage method which was first published in 1981.

Essentially Dosage requires five aptitudinal classifications to be assigned to each horse, specifically Brilliant, Intermediate, Classic, Solid, and Professional. These groups cover the complete spectrum of speed from sprinting ability to stamina. The influence the sire has on its progeny can be seen from this set of figures. However, to create the full Dosage Profile it is necessary to generate the same information for four generations of the pedigree. Each profile is based on a small predetermined list of sires.

These "Chef-De-Race" stallions have been selected based on the degree of consistency with which they pass specific traits on to their progeny. Combining these sets of figures is a simple matter of addition with the modification that for each successive generation the influence is halved. For instance the Dosage profile for the 2003 Arc winner Dalakhani is: 5-2-11-2-6.

From a Dosage profile it is possible to estimate the most suitable racing distance for the horse by using the Dosage Index. This ratio is simply the points assigned to the speed side of the profile to the points awarded to the stamina side. In other words the sum of the Brilliant points, Intermediate points and one-half of the Classic points divided by the total of one-half of the Classic points plus the Solid points plus Professional points. As an example a Dosage profile of 11-6-26-1-2 would result in a Dosage Index of 1.875.

The higher the Dosage Index the more likely the horse is to be suited to sprint distances: The average Dosage Index for 5F winners is approximately 4.6, whereas the equivalent figure for 12F horses is 2.0. The Dosage Index for the middle-distance champion Dalakhani is 0.93 and for the top sprinter Dayjur the figure is 2.85. These figures are significantly different from the averages illustrating the approximate nature of this approach and the degree of variance in the results.

Predicting Suitable Racing Distances from Pedigrees

The Dosage Index provides an approximation of the likely distance a horse will be suited by, but finding the four generations of pedigree is sometimes not straightforward, and there may be simpler methods that can be employed using information taken from just the sire and dam's sire. Furthermore there is an element of double-counting involved with the Dosage calculation on the sire's side of the pedigree. The traits passed to the offspring are identified by the sire, however, the Dosage method requires the aggregate of the dosage profiles of the sire, the sire's sire and so on for four generations. This would appear to over-emphasise this side of the pedigree. Also the Chef-De-Race list is relatively small which may lead to Dosage profiles based on only a few sires that would be less reliable.

A possible alternative is to analyse the progeny of the sire and generate an average winning distance. This would then be the estimate for all progeny. However, there are several weaknesses with this approach. Firstly, the results would produce a single estimate for each horse with the same sire which is particularly imprecise and would not distinguish between the progeny of two stayers (i.e. the sire and dam) and a stayer and a sprinter. Secondly the optimal race distance for a horse varies with age. As a rule the optimal racing distance increases as the horse gets older. This feature would not be fully accounted for by such a general approach. Thirdly, the average winning distance may not be the best measure. Normally the median winning distance figure is quoted since this is less susceptible to single wins over extreme distances although prolific winners may bias the estimate.

As an alternative the model proposed here is based on information collected from the sire and the dam's sire. It has been suggested that the main influence on stamina is the number of mitochondria available in the muscle tissue, and that mitochondrial DNA is inherited only through the female line. Consequently the best guide could well lie in an examination of the offspring of the dam. However, the main problem with this approach is lack of data. The progeny of each dam will be far less than of the sire making any statistical conclusions difficult to justify in a rigorous and reliable manner. Consequently, for this approach the maximum winning distance achieved by the three-year-old progeny of each sire is deduced and a mean average taken. Using just three-year-olds removes the problem associated with optimal distances changing with age. Taking just one figure from each offspring also reduces the impact of a prolific runner, and using the maximum fixes the distance at the end of the distance distribution for each horse making the averaging effect more reliable.

To construct the model, data taken from the 1995 to 2001 seasons were analysed and average maximum winning distances for the top sires derived. Sires with fewer than five winning offspring were omitted for obvious reasons. As an example, Sadler's Wells, one of the most influential sires, has an average maximum winning distance (AMWD) figure of 10.95 furlongs based on 156 horses. In contrast the AMWD for the three-year-old progeny of Puissance over this period was just 6.94 furlongs.

To forecast the likely winning distance of the progeny of any of these sires is it necessary to construct a simple model that takes the data pairs (i.e. the AMWD for the sire and dam's sire) and predicts the maximum winning distance of the offspring. Given the form of the data and the requirement of the model, the most obvious approach is to use regression analysis.

For each horse an AMWD is assigned to its sire and dam's sire. These figures, for as many horses as possible, are compared to the maximum winning distance for each three-year-old offspring, and the relationship recorded. For instance an observation may look like the following: for a horse with a maximum winning distance at age three of 9 furlongs sired by Sadler's Wells out of a dam sired by Puissance:

11.0	*6.9*	*9.0*
(Sadler's Wells AMWD)	*(Puissance AMWD)*	*MWD of progeny*

Similar records were calculated from the 1995-2001 data set on which to base the model. The best linear regression model that fitted the data is given next:

Maximum Winning = -0.1675 + 0.76*Sire's AMWD + 0.24*Dam Sire's AMWD Distance of Progeny

The coefficients of the model are statistically significant at the 95% level indicating that both are related to the forecast variable and that this relationship is unlikely to be created purely by chance.

The model above can be used to estimate the likely MWD for the progeny providing the sire and dam's sire's AMWD are known. In the example given earlier, a horse sired by Sadler's Wells out of a dam sired by Puissance would have an estimated MWD of approximately 10 furlongs. This figure is calculated as follows:

*Maximum Winning = -0.1675 + 0.76***10.95** *+ 0.24***6.94** *= 9.8 Distance of Progeny*

(*The figures in bold relate to the AMWDs for each sire.*)

The most interesting feature of this model is the ratio of the coefficients assigned to the variables. The Dosage approach recommends that for each successive generation the effect should be halved. If this applied to the model given above the coefficient for the sire's AMWD would be twice that of the dam's sires figure. However, in this model the ratio is three to one, indicating a much higher level of influence from the sire. Another interesting feature becomes apparent when the residuals of the model are analysed. The residuals are calculated by comparing the estimated MWD with the actual figures for the data used to construct the model. When analysed by the gender of the progeny the following results are produced:

Colt/Gelding or Filly	Average Residual	Total Residual
Colt/Gelding	-0.09	-114.6
Filly	0.09	114.6

Ideally these two values would be very close to zero, but this is far from the case. The implication of this result is that the model does not fully account for the gender of the offspring which would be the case for any model with a similar objective. This is a weakness that is easily overcome. One method that can be used is to add an additional variable to each observation used to construct the model indicating whether the horse is a colt/gelding or filly (i.e. 1 for a colt/gelding, 0 for a filly).

The model could then be redefined with an additional gender component. Unfortunately this new component would be a constant representing the average difference between the two sets of records for all race distances. If this constant was 0.5 furlongs, for instance, this would be the equivalent to an adjustment of 10% to a horse with a MWD of 5 furlongs but only 4% for middle distance horses. Clearly this is not an acceptable approach, so given the strong relationship between the MWD of the offspring and the AMWD of the sire, one alternative is to scale this constant by the AMWD. So for the previous example, a colt with a MWD of 9 furlongs, sired by Sadler's Well out of a dam sired by Puissance would have the following data: 11.0, 6.9, 11.0, 9.0, the second 11.0 represents the gender of the offspring. A filly would be represented by: 11.0, 6.9, 0, 9.0 (the zero indicates a filly). Using this representation produces the following model:

Maximum Winning
Distance of Progeny = 0.16 + 0.75*Sire's AMWD + 0.25*Dam Sire's AMWD
(Fillies)

Maximum Winning
Distance of Progeny = -0.16 + 0.75*Sire's AMWD + 0.25*Dam Sire's AMWD
(Colts/Geldings)   *+ 0.02*Sire's AMWD*

Naturally for the Colt/Gelding model the terms could be rationalised with the coefficient for the sire's AMWD increased to 0.77 and the final term removed. In the current form, though, it illustrates the differences between the two models more clearly. In order to check the applicability of the model a graph of its performance can be generated and analysed.

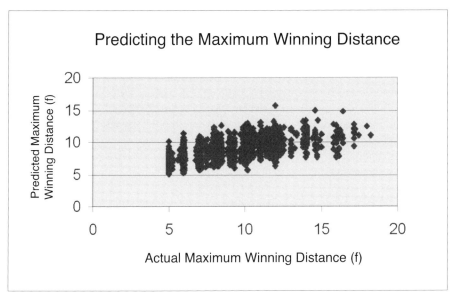

Figure 1: Model Performance

From Figure 1 it can be seen that whilst there is a definite positive correlation between the predicted and actual distances, there is a significant degree of variation throughout the range of distances. This degree of variation is due to the fact that the variables used do not fully explain the relationship between the pedigrees and the MWD which is empahsised by the correlation coefficient of 0.6. A similar distribution was found using the Dosage method and it can be easily explained.

The Dosage method, like this approach, can be used to estimate the likely maximum winning distance of horses, but on an individual basis is prone to error. To quote Steve Roman: "the confirmed relationship between pedigree type and performance applies technically only to large populations of runners and not necessarily to individuals, although the conclusions derived from the data may be considered as would any conclusions drawn from statistical studies."

In other words, whilst the method illustrates the underlying trends and is able to apply these well to large populations, for single observations there may be a large degree of difference between the predicted and actual distances. This is the case for the vast majority of real-world problems. Though an abstract statistical model can predict well in general, there is always going to be a degree of error for individual cases. Roman uses the excellent example of life expectancy and smoking. Whilst smoking reduces your life expectancy there are many smokers who live way beyond the statistical expectancy. Notwithstanding these reservations, it is clear the model can be used to predict the likely maximum winning distance of horses.

Results Summary

In order to more rigorously test the effectiveness of this method a sample of 2452 race performances was extracted from the 2002 season. These performances represented 334 races and were confined to three-year-old horses only. The success rate for these runners was 11.2% and a level £1 staked on each would have returned a loss at starting price of 19p/£1 staked.

The predicted Maximum Winning Distances were calculated for each horse in the data set and compared to the distance over which the animal raced. Horses which had a predicted maximum winning distance less than the race distance won 10.0% of races and returned a loss at starting price of 32p per £1 staked. Those running over a distance within their predicted stamina capabilities (i.e. a predicted maximum winning distance greater than the race distance) won 12.1% of races and returned a loss of just 8p for every £1 staked. Clearly these horses are better betting propositions.

For the first three months of the season, the success rate of horses running at distances beyond the predicted maximum distance drops to 9% and the betting loss increases to 39p per £1 staked.

An examination of the differences between the predicted maximum winning distances and the actual distances also proved informative with horses running at a distance three furlongs or more further than the predicted measure winning just 6% of races and returning a huge loss of 65p for every £1 staked at starting price. There appears to be an advantage to following horses which the model indicates are likely to be suited to the race distance.

An Alternative Approach to Distance Prediction – The Distance Profile

The Dosage method uses a distribution of values associated with different categories of speed or stamina. Thus the influence of the sire is easily visible and the relative influences of the different components of the dosage calculation can be compared. It is possible to create a similar profile without using what may appear to be arbitrary values. The method proposed here is to analyse the performances of the offspring and generate a profile based on the ratio of these historical successes in the following form:

Sprint Wins – Mile Wins – Middle Distance Wins – Staying Wins

Such a classification would have four numerical values illustrating the proportion of progeny which have a maximum winning distance classified by each category. As an example the profile for Sadler's Wells, using this scheme, is 2-16-73-9. From this profile it can be seen that the vast majority of Sadler's Wells's three-year-old progeny have a MWD in the middle distance category. And only 2% have a MWD in the sprint group. Although using the previous approach the AMWD for Sadler's Wells of 10.95 indicates that his progeny are best run at middle distances it does not provide the same depth of information as this representation.

Before such a method can be implemented it is necessary to determine the distance categories. The obvious method is to simply divide the race distances into convenient exclusive groups such as 5-6F, 6.1-9F, etc. However, a horse that has a MWD of 5.95F would be placed in the Sprint category and one with a MWD of 6.1 would be placed in the Mile group. Given the closeness of these two horses it seems incorrect to place them in different groups. The preferred solution is to adopt a technique used in Fuzzy Set Theory and overlap the distance categories, for instance 5-7F, 6.5-9.5F etc. Therefore a horse could feature in two classifications, such as the Sprint and Mile groups, with the resulting distribution likely to be smoother and more representative of the progeny. After an amount of research the following classifications were found to give the best results:

Classification	Minimum Distance	Maximum Distance
Sprint	5.0F	7.0F
Mile	6.5F	9.5F
Middle Distance	9.0F	13.0F
Staying	12.5F	17.5F

The profiles can easily be calculated for each sire then normalised to produce proportions expressed as percentages.

Though such profiles are useful when examining sires, given the influence of the dam's side of the pedigree they do not provide a single profile for the offspring. In order to generate a profile for the progeny of a known sire and dam's sire using the distance profiles it is necessary to combine these two sets of figures to form a single profile. From previous analysis the degrees of influence for the sire and dam's sire were found to be approximately 0.75 and 0.25 so to combine two groups is simply a matter of applying these fractions to each group in turn then summing the new proportions. For example, calculating the Distance Profile for a horse sired by Sadler's Wells out of a mare sired by Puissance would require the following calculation:

Sadler's Wells Profile:	*2-16-73-9*	*reduced by 0.75 gives:*	*1.5-12.0-54.8-6.8*
Puissance Profile:	*51-38-10-0*	*reduced by 0.25 gives:*	*12.8-9.5-2.5-0.0*
Sadler's Wells-Puissance Profile:	**14-22-57-7**		

Though Sadler's Wells has a strong influence towards middle distances the dam side of this pedigree has a speed influence resulting in a profile that predicts 14% of the three-year-old offspring will have a MWD in the 5-7 furlong range. Naturally it is possible to generate a single figure estimate, as in the previous method, from this profile by simply scaling each proportion by the mid-point of the category then dividing by 100. For this example the figure is 9.92F.

Estimating Ability from Pedigrees

"To get the best, breed the best to the best" is a well-worn racing cliché, but there is more than a degree of truth to this concept. Every season the yearling sales will boast horses that fetch hundreds of thousands of pounds and others that will pass through the ring for a few hundred. The main reason behind this is the pedigree. The best sires not only pass to the offspring such traits as a preference for certain distances and racing surfaces, but also ability. This goes some way to explain why the progeny of such sires as Sadler's Wells and Northern Dancer have dominated Group racing in recent years.

Assessing the likely ability of unraced horses is naturally of great benefit to breeders and prospective owners, but the advantage to bettors is not as clear until one turns to two-year-old races. These events are often contested by horses with no previous racing experience which makes the task of race analysis more complex. However, this additional obfuscation of the form can be used to the bettor's advantage.

Bookmakers also need to assess the race and are faced with the same problems as the bettors, and this additional degree of difficulty gives the well-informed bettor a considerable advantage. Knowledge of pedigrees and training patterns will almost certainly generate the bettor a profit during the course of the year.

The Dosage method provides an assessment of the likely ability of a runner via the total number of dosage points the animal is awarded. The more points the better the animal is likely to be. However, this type of numerical assessment is difficult to interpret when used for ability. Unlike the previous section where the result is a distance, it is not straightforward to relate a dosage total to ability.

For instance, a figure of 20 would be considered better than 18, but by how much? Would the 20-rated horse be Group class, and the 18-rated animal only be expected to achieve Listed winning status? And how would well-bred horses from sires not included in the Chef-De-Race list be assessed? Such animals would have relatively low dosage totals even though their expectations would be far greater than the raw figures indicate.

As an alternative the handicap marks achieved by the offspring of the sires could be analysed in the same way as the maximum winning distances in the previous research. However, a preferred solution is to use the profiling technique to generate a more informative race-type profile for the offspring similar to the distance profile.

To construct such a model it is first necessary to generate a race-type classification. The recommended form is to divide races into the following groups: Group 1, Other Class A races, Class B and C races, Class D races, Class E, F and G races. For the offspring of each sire the best win, in terms of this classification, is recorded with the resultant profile normalised to represent percentages. For example the profiles for Sadler's Wells and Puissance are:

Percentage of Best Wins at Three-years-Old

Sire	Group 1	Class A	Class BC	Class D	Class EFG
Sadler's Wells Winners Profile	5	14	18	60	3
Puissance Winners Profile	0	3	9	30	58

From these individual profiles it can be seen that 5% of Sadler's Well's winning progeny won Group 1 races at age three and 30% of the winning progeny of Puissance could at best achieve a Class D success. When comparing the offspring of these two sires it is apparent from the profiles that the Sadler's Wells horse would be more likely to win a Group 1 race and that the Puissance horse will most likely be contesting the lower grades of race.

Such an assessment ignores the influence from the dam side of the pedigree. This is easily resolved by using the weighting method from the distance research. So if a horse had Sadler's Wells as a sire and a dam sired by Puissance the combined Ability Profile would be:

Sadler's Wells Profile:	5-14-18-60-3	reduced by 0.75 gives:	3.8-10.5-13.5-45.0-2.2
Puissance Profile:	0-3-9-30-58	reduced by 0.25 gives:	0.0-0.8-2.2-7.5-14.5
Sadler's Wells-Puissance Profile:	**4-11-16-52-17**		

From the ability profile it can be seen that the horse would have a 15% chance of winning a Class A race (including Group 1 races), but a 69% likelihood of rising no farther than Class D. The more heavily the profile is weighted towards the Group 1 and Class A races the more ability the horse is likely to possess.

Though this method provides a profile for each runner, it can be reduced to a single figure comparable to the dosage points total by scaling the profile by appropriate weights. To generate these weights it is necessary to formulate a basis for their scale. On method is to use the BHB handicap marks. Using this data, an average winning handicap mark can be calculated for each race type classification which can then be used to convert the profile into a single figure measure, or an Ability Score. From an analysis of five years data, the following weights were deduced: Group 1: 115; Class A: 100; Class BC: 85; Class D: 70; Class EFG: 55. Applying these weights to the Sadler's Well-Puissance profile given earlier produces an ability score of 75. The calculation is detailed next:

Race Class	Profile	Weight	Total (Profile * Weight)
Group 1	4	115	460
Other Class A races	11	100	1100
Class B & C	16	85	1360
Class D	52	70	3640
Class EFG	17	55	935
Total			7495

Ability Score = 7495/100 = 74.95

A score over 75 would indicate a well-bred animal possible capable of running against the best, whereas a score of 65 or lower would indicate that successes are likely to be found at the lower end of the racing scale.

Results Summary

In order to validate this method, a data set consisting of 2452 performances by three-year-olds was sampled and the ability scores for each runner based on the weighting procedure given in the previous section were calculated. The lowest score attributed to a horse was 56 and the highest was 83. The test data contained 24 Group 1 wins, 158 other Class A successes, 456 Class BC wins, 1020 Class D wins and 794 Class EFG successes.

The 24 Group 1 winners all had an ability score of 70 or higher, and 156 of the 158 other Class A winners had an ability score over 65, with 134 of these scoring over 70. Of those rated 80+, 28% won a Class A race, with only one failing to score higher than a Class EFG event. 62% of the horses rated less than 65 could manage only a Class EFG victory at best. The best win by a horse rated less than 60 was a Class D (one horse), the remaining successes came in the lowest class races.

These results show that the pedigree assessment is highly correlated with ability at three-years-old and hence could become a useful method for assessing the likely prospects of unraced horses as well as two-year-olds with Classic aspirations.

Conclusions

Dosage is an accepted method for analysing pedigrees and predicting ability and distance suitability. However, the approach has several major weaknesses. Firstly, only a small sample of sires is examined in order to make the Dosage assessment, consequently the influence of the vast majority of sires is simply ignored. Secondly, in the light of new research, the method of halving the level of influence for each generation appears flawed. Finally, the Dosage Profile and points total are not easily interpreted.

In this article two methods have been proposed which can be used to predict the maximum winning distance for three-year-old progeny using just the sire and dam's sire. The test results are very encouraging and indicate that the models are valid. Whilst the first method generates a single distance estimate, the modification which leads to a more informative prediction in the form of the Distance Profile is particularly interesting. Since it is based on percentages, the profile is easily assimilated with the likely suitable distances apparent from the distribution. The profile also highlights sires with limited influence. For these horses the profile will be uniform across the distance categories.

The Ability Score is equivalent to the total Dosage Points and from the results it appears to discriminate well between those horses likely to reach the top level of racing and the remainder. For instance the ability score for Rock of Gibraltar was 78, for Hawk Wing the score was also 78 and for High Chaparral the figure was 81. Based on this information these horses were destined to reach the top. The Ability Profile can be used to supplement the ability score and provide a clear illustration of the likelihood of a horse reaching a specific race standard as a three-year-old.

Naturally performing the necessary calculations in order to generate the profiles will be quite time-consuming. However, the website www.sireform.com presents this information on a daily basis for all British Flat races.

CHAPTER 5
FLAT HANDICAP RACES – GENERATING
AN ELIMINATION METHOD

Some commentators believe that handicaps were designed to make racing more competitive and more exciting for the racing public. Other, perhaps more enlightened commentators, believe that handicaps were created to simply increase bookmakers' profits. However, they do make up a significant proportion of Flat racing so deserve our attention, even if it is felt that they will not be the most profitable betting medium.

Approaches to Solving Non-Juvenile Handicap Races

There are many possible solutions to the problem of finding the winners of handicap races. Unfortunately using Form Ratings is not one of them. In the mid-1990s I monitored the performance of one of the main ratings providers for two complete Flat seasons. Whilst the ratings performed reasonably well in general, the performance in non-juvenile handicaps was extremely poor. In fact the success rate of the top-rated horses was no better than could be achieved by selecting the runners on a random basis. In other words as many winners could be found in these races using the trusted pin sticking approach.

But why should the ratings perform so poorly for one particular race class? The answer is concerned with the way these ratings are calculated. The BHB awards ratings to every horse and these are used to generate the handicap. Form Ratings are created using the same approach, so unless the private handicapper is far better than the BHB's team of handicappers these ratings will never perform well. Speed figures, on the other hand, may offer a profitable method. Though speed figures calculated in the conventional way, using standard times and going allowances, are unlikely to produce consistent profits, recent innovations in the calculation of speed figures, where standard times and not used, are producing more accurate assessments which could well return a profit from these particularly difficult races.

Other possible solutions include selecting horses with respect to their starting stall. Some courses have heavy biases across the width of the track either due to the way water is retained in the soil or, more simply, by the configuration of the track. It is possible to highlight biases from an analysis of historical races which can then be used as a selection method. For instance the Beverley 5 furlong course has an extreme bias to the high drawn horses and in non-juvenile handicaps the winner will often be drawn high. Trainer trends offer another possible solution. Some trainers have very definite patterns to placing their horses and many can be followed profitably in handicap races. Another possible solution uses an approach based on eliminating horses from the race, details of this method are given in the following sections.

Developing an Elimination Method

As the name suggests, an Elimination Method is based on eliminating horses with little or no chance of success to reduce the field to a more manageable size. An efficient elimination approach will use the variables which have the greatest impact on the result of the race to reduce the field size to a handful of runners. For the majority of race types the most important factor is ability. Consequently an elimination technique would first remove all horses which appear to lack the ability to win the race. However, for handicaps the range of ability possessed by the runners has been normalised by the weights the horses are set to carry, and as such this factor is of limited use. This is illustrated by the poor performance of ratings for these races discussed earlier.

A more important variable is recent form. The Official Handicapper reacts very quickly to horses in form by raising their handicap marks. However, he/she is often slow to react to horses that are out of form. Consequently these horses will remain on a similar mark for some time and as a result will be unlikely to win. Assessing recent form is not straightforward, but one simple guide is the recent finishing positions of the horses. Tables 1-3 present the success rates by previous finishing positions for turf handicap races staged over the three seasons 2000-02. In each table unplaced refers to horses that finished outside the first three.

Table 1: Success Rate of Turf Non-Juvenile Handicap Runners by Finishing Position on Latest Start

Finishing Position	Wins	Runs	Success Rate %	Average Return/£1
First	811	5761	14.1%	-£0.17
Second	646	5249	12.3%	-£0.19
Third	542	5356	10.1%	-£0.20
Other	2513	44980	5.6%	-£0.33
All	4512	61346	7.4%	-£0.29

Table 2: Success Rate of Turf Non-Juvenile Handicap Runners by Finishing Position Two Runs Ago

Finishing Position	Wins	Runs	Success Rate %	Average Return/£1
First	669	5984	11.2%	-£0.16
Second	564	5547	10.2%	-£0.22
Third	472	5510	8.6%	-£0.24
Other	2807	44305	6.3%	-£0.33
All	4512	61346	7.4%	-£0.29

Table 2: Success Rate of Turf Non-Juvenile Handicap Runners by Finishing Position Three Runs Ago

Finishing Position	Wins	Runs	Success Rate %	Average Return/£1
First	542	5961	9.1%	-£0.26
Second	517	5608	9.2%	-£0.24
Third	499	5694	8.8%	-£0.17
Other	2954	44083	6.7%	-£0.32
All	4512	61346	7.4%	-£0.29

The average loss for these races is 29% (29p for every £1 staked), which is the bookmakers' average over-round for handicap races. The overall strike rate of 7% implies that the average field size for the races examined was approximately fourteen. Consequently the average loss per runner is approximately 2p, or 2% in terms of over-round. This compares very well with most sports betting. For instance the average over-round for football betting is 4% per outcome (win, lose or draw) which is extremely high and very difficult for the average punter to beat.

At this point many readers will be thinking that finishing positions alone are not adequate. What about horses that were beaten less than one length into fourth, compared to those beaten 20 lengths? What about movements in race types, from non-handicap races to handicap events? What about horses from stables which were out of form and are now in form? All of these criticisms are valid and more sophisticated methods can be developed (see Utilising Recent Trainer Form for alternative approaches). However, for the purposes of this elimination method finishing positions are adequate. From the three tables it can be seen that each run has a different level of impact on the race result. For horses that won on their latest run the chance of success is 14.1%, whereas for those that won three runs ago this figure is 9.1%. The degree of importance of these three factors can be illustrated easily by a graph (Graph 1). The greater the gradient of the lines linking the four positions the greater the impact of the variable on the outcome of the race. Clearly the most recent run is of greatest importance. Given the difference between the levels of impact of each run it is more productive to examine the finishing positions in triples as detailed in Table 4.

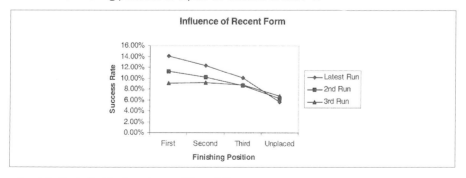

Graph 1: Illustrating the Importance of Recent Form

Table 4: Success Rate and Return for Horses Running in Non-Juvenile Turf Handicap Races 2000-2002

Finishing Positions	Wins	Runs	Success Rate %	Average Return/£1
121	24	117	20.5%	-£0.07
221	33	164	20.1%	+£0.16
211	32	165	19.4%	-£0.22
222	21	111	18.9%	+£0.25
111	32	175	18.3%	-£0.23
331	17	95	17.9%	+£0.26
311	23	129	17.8%	-£0.22
012	63	376	16.8%	+£0.15
223	16	96	16.7%	+£0.06
112	23	139	16.5%	-£0.01
131	14	85	16.5%	-£0.31
122	16	98	16.3%	-£0.06
301	48	310	15.5%	+£0.05
312	14	93	15.1%	-£0.23
322	14	93	15.1%	-£0.05
333	12	80	15.0%	+£0.34
202	42	289	14.5%	-£0.01
313	14	97	14.4%	+£0.07
011	72	499	14.4%	-£0.32
031	62	445	13.9%	-£0.13
132	12	88	13.6%	-£0.29
231	15	110	13.6%	-£0.27
022	53	390	13.6%	-£0.09
201	43	323	13.3%	-£0.10
021	67	514	13.0%	-£0.28
023	49	379	12.9%	-£0.09
321	16	124	12.9%	-£0.36
001	270	2156	12.5%	-£0.17
232	10	80	12.5%	-£0.38
212	13	105	12.4%	-£0.39
101	43	350	12.3%	-£0.20
302	40	327	12.2%	-£0.16
213	13	114	11.4%	-£0.30

Table 4: *continued*

Finishing Positions	Wins	Runs	Success Rate %	Average Return/£1
303	40	357	11.2%	-£0.06
002	254	2283	11.1%	-£0.22
133	9	81	11.1%	-£0.33
033	40	362	11.0%	+£0.04
203	33	299	11.0%	-£0.18
013	37	336	11.0%	-£0.25
110	54	517	10.4%	-£0.08
032	38	365	10.4%	-£0.40
210	61	587	10.4%	+£0.00
123	8	82	9.8%	-£0.27
103	36	377	9.5%	-£0.33
233	7	75	9.3%	-£0.31
113	10	110	9.1%	-£0.53
130	37	413	9.0%	-£0.03
310	39	447	8.7%	+£0.06
003	213	2445	8.7%	-£0.24
102	28	330	8.5%	-£0.52
320	30	364	8.2%	-£0.18
010	169	2095	8.1%	-£0.25
323	5	66	7.6%	-£0.50
120	33	443	7.4%	-£0.28
220	29	390	7.4%	-£0.33
020	150	2116	7.1%	-£0.30
330	28	397	7.1%	-£0.29
100	163	2556	6.4%	-£0.31
030	150	2386	6.3%	-£0.27
332	5	82	6.1%	-£0.45
300	154	2633	5.8%	-£0.25
200	133	2334	5.7%	-£0.35
000	1267	26936	4.7%	-£0.38
230	16	366	4.4%	-£0.54
All	4512	61346	7.4%	-£0.29

† *For each form triple the most recent run is furthest to the right.*

Table 4 shows the number of wins, runs, success rate and average return for the 64 different combinations. A race performance outside the first three is indicated by a zero.

From Table 4 it can be calculated that horses which have failed to make the frame on any of their last three starts constitute 44% of all runners, yet win at a rate of less than one in twenty. The highest success rate for any single form category is 20.5%, almost three times the average, with only one other category recording an average win rate of over 20%.

The linearity associated with form is detectable from this table. As the form figures improve, the chance of success increases. However, this does not mean the profit will increase. Though the relationship between form and success rate is linear, the association between form and profit is non-linear. This is why the horses with the best form (i.e. 111) do not yield the best return to the punter. A list of the profitable form categories is given in Table 5.

Table 5: Profitable Form Categories

Form Category†	Wins	Runs	Success Rate %	Average Return/£1
333	12	80	15.0%	+£0.34
331	17	95	17.9%	+£0.26
222	21	111	18.9%	+£0.25
221	33	164	20.1%	+£0.16
012	63	376	16.8%	+£0.15
313	14	97	14.4%	+£0.07
310	39	447	8.7%	+£0.06
223	16	96	16.7%	+£0.06
301	48	310	15.5%	+£0.05
033	40	362	11.0%	+£0.04
210	61	587	10.4%	∣£0.00
All	364	2725	13.4%	+£0.08

† For each form triple the most recent run is furthest to the right.

Simply omitting those horses which were unplaced on each of their last three starts does improve the success rate and return. The 61,346 horses are reduced to 34,410, which includes 3,245 winners, a success rate of 9.4% and a loss of 22p for every £1 staked. This is given in Table 6, together with three other potential elimination rules and the results for the horses remaining after the rule has been applied.

Table 6: Eliminations based on Recent Form

Eliminations	Wins	Runs	Success Rate %	Average Return/£1
Omitting horses with a 000 form line	3245	34410	9%	-£0.22
Omitting all horses which have not won in last three races	1663	15245	11%	-£0.20
Omitting horses unplaced on any of their last three races	428	2854	15%	-£0.16
Leaving just horses placed on each run without winning	90	683	13%	-£0.10

Although recent form is a useful elimination variable, an equally important factor is course absence. The number of days a horse has been off the course is often used in systems and it is not difficult to justify when there exists such a high correlation between the gap between races and the success rate. However, this factor becomes even more useful when combined with a time-of-year variable. Table 7 shows the success rate of handicappers by the course absence and time of year.

Table 7: Success Rate by Course Absence and Time of Year

Days Since Last Run	March-May		June-August		September-November		All Months	
	Success Rate%	Average Return/£1	Success Rate%	Average Return/£1	Success Rate%	Average Return/£1	Success Rate%	Average Return/£1
1-7	9.8%	-£0.11	10.4%	-£0.20	8.0%	-£0.22	9.9%	-£0.18
8-14	7.1%	-£0.32	8.2%	-£0.31	7.2%	-£0.30	7.8%	-£0.31
15-28	7.0%	-£0.30	7.9%	-£0.29	6.4%	-£0.29	7.4%	-£0.29
29-60	6.6%	-£0.23	6.9%	-£0.30	5.1%	-£0.38	6.4%	-£0.31
61-100	6.2%	-£0.04	6.5%	-£0.27	4.3%	-£0.51	5.7%	-£0.30
101+	4.6%	-£0.43	4.8%	-£0.28	3.4%	-£0.44	4.5%	-£0.39
All Days	6.6%	-£0.31	8.1%	-£0.28	6.3%	-£0.32	7.4%	-£0.29

Essentially the number of days a horse has been absent from the course is reflected in the success rate of the animal. The longer the course absence the less likely the horse is to win. However, the pricing appears to take this into account except for the extremes. The average loss is around 30p for every £1 staked, but this drops to just 18p for horse returning within 7 days and increases to almost 40p for horse off the course for 100 days or more. This needs to be reflected in any elimination approach.

Horses returning from a course absence of 101 days or more win at a rate of approximately 4.5%, this compares to an average figure of 7.4%. And towards the end of the season horses off the track for 29 days or more score at a rate lower than the average. Clearly these could be included in the elimination process.

A third variable that is often overlooked when analysing these races is the price the horse started on its previous start. Table 8 presents the success rate of handicappers by their starting price on the previous run.

Table 8: Success Rate by Price on Previous Start

Price On Latest Run	Wins	Runs	Success Rate %	Average Return/£1
Odds On	63	510	12.4%	-£0.17
Ev-2/1	236	1860	12.7%	-£0.07
9/4-4/1	563	5926	9.5%	-£0.28
9/2-9/1	1368	16306	8.4%	-£0.26
10/1-16/1	1357	18968	7.2%	-£0.27
18/1-33/1	816	14663	5.6%	-£0.37
40/1+	109	3113	3.5%	-£0.47
All	4512	61346	7.4%	-£0.29

Whilst the starting price of a horse is a good indicator to its chance of winning, from Table 8 it appears that the price the horse started on its previous run is also a good indicator. As the price increases the chance of winning diminishes, and the average loss per bet increases. Whilst the price a horse starts at is influenced by many factors, a key element is the number of runners in the race. The larger the field size the greater the likelihood of the horse starting at a bigger price. So a horse starting at 12/1 in a four-runner race is not equivalent to a horse starting at the same price in a 30-runner event.

To remove the effect of the field size on the price, one simple method is to divide the starting price by the number of runners in the race to create a Price Ratio. So for a horse starting at 12/1 in a four runner race the price ratio would be: 12/4 = 3.00. A 12/1 shot in a 30-runner race would have the price ratio of: 12/30=0.4. The success rate of horses compared to their previous race price ratio is given in Table 9.

Table 9: Success Rate by the Previous Race Price Ratio

Previous Race Price Ratio	Wins	Runs	Success Rate %	Average Return/£1
0..0.25	519	4437	11.7%	-£0.18
0.26..0.50	1102	12143	9.1%	-£0.23
0.51..0.75	924	11493	8.0%	-£0.24
0.76..1.00	706	10083	7.0%	-£0.32
1.01..1.50	637	10161	6.3%	-£0.30
1.51..2.00	324	5643	5.7%	-£0.34
2.01..2.50	128	2527	5.1%	-£0.42
2.51..3.00	74	1686	4.4%	-£0.48
3.01..3.50	25	787	3.2%	-£0.50
3.51..4.00	22	669	3.3%	-£0.61
4.01+	51	1717	3.0%	-£0.46
All	4512	61346	7.4%	-£0.29

As the previous race price ratio increases, the likelihood of success diminishes and the average loss increases, which can easily be used to generate an elimination rule. For example eliminating all horses with a previous race price ratio of 2.01 or higher would remove 7,386 runners including 300 winners (success rate: 4%). The loss associated with these runners would be approximately 47p for every £1 staked, significantly higher than the average of 29p.

Implementing an Elimination Method

The simplest way to use an elimination method is to identify a set of elimination criteria and apply it to the races under analysis. For example, the elimination rules may take the following form:

Eliminate all horses which:
* Were unplaced on both of their last two runs
* Have been unraced for 100 days or more
* Have been unraced for more than 29 days for races run in September to November
* Have a previous race price ratio of 2.5 or higher

Once identified it is a straightforward task to apply these rules to any race. The result will be to reduce the race to a more manageable size in terms of runners and make it easier to analyse using conventional techniques.

An alternative approach is to identify a compound rule based on the elimination criteria and then apply this to each runner. However, of the three factors covered previously two are related. The starting price of a horse is linked to its finishing position, so the form, as indicated by the finishing position, is related to the previous race price ratio. Consequently including these two factors in a single elimination rule is not straightforward.

From the analyses it is apparent that as the form figures increase in magnitude the chance of success reduces. So one simple approach is to base the rule on the aggregate of the three finishing positions. Naturally an upper limit for each position needs to be set, a suggested level is 10. This means that a finishing position outside the first 10 would be fixed at ten. Using the approach, the lowest the aggregate form figure could reach is three (three consecutive wins) and the highest is 30.

Including the days since last run factor with this aggregate figure is not straightforward. Simply adding the two would mean that for most cases the influence of the form factor would be extremely diluted by the course absence figure due to the differences in the range of these two variables. Whilst the aggregate form figure has an upper limit of 30, the limit for the course absence factor could well exceed 1,000.

Alternatively, the two values can be multiplied together, this preserves the influence of each. The resultant Form and Days value will range from a lower limit of 3 (three consecutive wins with the latest race run the previous day) to over 30,000. It is then possible to analyse these values to determine a threshold to use as the elimination rule. Using the data from 2000-2002 the optimal threshold appears to be 100, so the elimination rule becomes: Eliminate all horses with a Form and Days value exceeding 100. It should be noted that using 100 as the threshold means that any horse that has been off the course for more than 33 will be eliminated.

Applying this rule to all races reduces the number of runners from 61,346 to 7,477, increases the win rate from just over 7% to over 13%, and reduces the loss from 29p/£1 to 7p/£1. Interestingly the Form and Days figure can be used as a form of rating to rank the horses in order. For the 2000-02 data selecting the horse with the lowest Form and Days rating, providing it is below 100, produces the following results: 553 winners from 3482 selections, a success rate of 16%, and an average return of 6p/£1.

However, this method applies the same level of influence to each form figure. From Tables 1-3 it is clear that the latest race has the most influence on the result, so this approach needs to be modified to take account of this feature. Analysing the data in Tables 1-3 indicates that the latest race performance is twice as important as the second latest run. And this result is 2.5 times as influential as the third most recent run. To include this information in the calculation of the Form and Days figure is simply a matter of applying these three factors to the form figures before multiplying by the course absence value. As an example, consider a horse which has been unraced for 24 days and has the following form figures 823:

Adjusted Form and Days Value = (8+2.5*2+5*3)*24 = 672

Based on the 2000-02 data set, horses which have an Adjusted Form and Days value of no more than 100 won 254 races from 1385 selections, a success rate of just over 18%, slightly better than the strike rate for the unadjusted value and significantly higher than the random expectation of 7%. In terms of profit, backing the horse with the lowest Adjusted Form and Days value, providing it was less than 100, returned a profit of just over 6%, very similar to the equivalent unadjusted figure.

The options for elimination rules are endless. Whilst a selection of possible factors have been analysed in this article, there are many more that could be included. For instance, the age of the horse could be added to the procedure with older animals eliminated, the distance beaten could replace form figures, and the number of runs since the horse won could be added to the final rule set. Whichever set of factors are chosen the approach will remain the same and the results should make the additional analysis worthwhile.

CHAPTER 6
ALL WEATHER DEBUTANTS

All Weather racing is far from an ideal medium for punters looking to profit. The competitive nature of the races combined with the changing draw bias, inconsistent horses, problems in running and high bookmakers' over-rounds make the task of winning very difficult. There is also the added difficulty of assessing horses that have turf form but are new to the artificial surface.

Evaluating the likelihood of success of horses which are new to the All Weather racing is not straightforward; it has been suggested that the best approach is to simply ignore them since they very rarely win. There is plenty of evidence to support this seemingly extreme solution. During the 2000-2002 seasons, the success rate of All Weather debutants was a lowly 8% with an average loss to the level stake starting price punter of 36p/£1. However, a rule which just eliminates all horses without experience of the surface is rather simplistic and easily improved upon. Table 1 shows the performance of two-year-olds running for the first time on the All Weather. Those making their racecourse debut (i.e. those without any racing experience on any surface) during the three years 2000-2002 won at a rate of 9.5% but returned a loss at starting price of 54p for every £1 staked. This is a staggering loss, competing with the National Lottery in terms of value and making these horses difficult to support.

Horses which have already raced on the turf are better betting propositions, especially those which have been assessed and allotted a rating by the BHB Handicapper. Though the loss for experienced runners that have not been rated remains high at 46p/£1, the figure for those which have a BHB handicap mark drops to just 18p/£1. Clearly these are the horses to note.

Interestingly, a £1 staked at starting price on all rated juveniles making their All Weather debut in a selling contest returned a profit of 35p per bet, with a win rate of almost 14%. For all other non-handicap races a level stake profit is achieved by backing all newcomers rated 70 or higher, but for nurseries there appears to be little benefit in following any debut runner.

Table 2 shows similar statistics for non-juvenile races. Again a similar pattern exists, with horses making their racing debut offering very poor value with only 27 winners from 444 runners and a level stake loss of 61p/£1. For those with racecourse experience the loss improves to just 43p/£1, and then to 26p/31 for rated horses.

For runners in claiming races the minimum rating threshold appears to be 60, with horses rated higher than this figure returning a profit in the past. For handicaps this threshold needs to be increased to 80.

All Weather debutants do not offer the best value betting medium, though simply to ignore them could be dangerous. From these tables it can be seen that by noting the BHB Turf rating for each newcomer it is possible to identify those with a greater chance of success, and for some race types this could form the basis of a profitable systematic approach.

Table 1: Analysis of First All Weather Runs: 2000-2002 – Juvenile Horses

Juvenile Races	Conditions Races			Claimers			Maidens			Sellers			Handicaps			All Races		
	Wins	Runs	Ret/£1	Wins	Runs	Ret/£1	Wins	Runs	Ret/£1	Wins	Runs	Ret/£1	Wins	Runs	Ret/£1	Wins	Runs	Ret/£1
Unraced on Any Surface	2	16	-£0.71	1	11	-£0.86	18	178	-£0.44	2	37	-£0.84	na	na	na	23	242	-£0.54
Raced but Unrated on Turf	9	92	-£0.37	4	62	-£0.79	86	873	-£0.43	19	251	-£0.58	8	102	-£0.34	126	1380	-£0.46
All Rated Horses	4	35	-£0.27	6	51	-£0.31	15	115	-£0.36	13	95	+£0.35	12	183	-£0.28	50	479	-£0.18
Turf Rating 40+	4	35	-£0.27	6	50	-£0.29	15	114	-£0.35	13	92	+£0.40	12	183	-£0.28	50	474	-£0.17
Turf Rating 50+	4	34	-£0.25	6	46	-£0.23	15	110	-£0.33	13	78	+£0.65	12	178	-£0.26	50	446	-£0.12
Turf Rating 60+	4	31	-£0.18	5	28	+£0.02	14	92	-£0.24	6	37	+£0.49	10	143	-£0.28	39	331	-£0.15
Turf Rating 70+	4	20	+£0.27	3	15	-£0.04	12	55	+£0.06	0	3	-£1.00	4	78	-£0.60	23	171	-£0.24
Turf Rating 80+	3	7	+£1.70	1	6	-£0.72	3	7	+£0.02	0	1	-£1.00	1	15	-£0.70	8	36	-£0.20

Table 2: Analysis of First All Weather Runs: 2000-2002 – Non-Juvenile Horses

Rating		Listed Races	Conditions Stks	Claimers	Maidens	Sellers	Handicaps	All Races
Unraced on Any Surface	Wins	0	3	0	20	1	3	27
	Runs	1	30	28	300	40	45	444
	Ave.Ret/£1	-£1.00	-£0.52	-£1.00	-£0.60	-£0.95	-£0.20	-£0.61
Unrated on Turf	Wins	0	4	1	67	3	20	95
	Runs	2	39	69	745	76	264	1195
	Ave.Ret/£1	-£1.00	-£0.23	-£0.70	-£0.46	-£0.75	-£0.18	-£0.43
All Rated Horses	Wins	2	10	12	37	8	119	188
	Runs	18	169	172	377	139	1746	2621
	Ave.Ret/£1	-£0.74	-£0.44	-£0.39	-£0.60	-£0.42	-£0.14	-£0.26
Turf Rating 30+	Wins	2	10	12	37	8	119	188
	Runs	18	168	163	374	136	1740	2599
	Ave.Ret/£1	-£0.74	-£0.43	-£0.36	-£0.60	-£0.41	-£0.14	-£0.25
Turf Rating 40+	Wins	2	10	12	37	8	117	186
	Runs	18	163	147	354	115	1685	2482
	Ave.Ret/£1	-£0.74	-£0.42	-£0.29	-£0.57	-£0.30	-£0.12	-£0.23
Turf Rating 50+	Wins	2	10	12	37	3	107	171
	Runs	18	150	106	291	79	1492	2136
	Ave.Ret/£1	-£0.74	-£0.37	-£0.02	-£0.48	-£0.79	-£0.10	-£0.20
Turf Rating 60+	Wins	2	10	12	35	3	76	138
	Runs	18	130	73	232	51	1033	1537
	Ave.Ret/£1	-£0.74	-£0.27	+£0.43	-£0.42	-£0.67	-£0.13	-£0.18
Turf Rating 70+	Wins	2	7	5	27	2	40	83
	Runs	18	65	29	140	23	571	846
	Ave.Ret/£1	-£0.74	+£0.02	+£0.11	-£0.32	-£0.40	-£0.14	-£0.17
Turf Rating 80+	Wins	2	3	3	4	1	16	29
	Runs	18	29	11	18	10	194	280
	Ave.Ret/£1	-£0.74	-£0.38	+£0.56	-£0.23	+£0.00	+£0.12	+£0.00

BETTING STRATEGIES
CHAPTER 1: EXPLOITING HISTORICAL TRAINER TRENDS

If all racehorse trainers used the same training methods and race planning approaches there would be no need for the punter to consider the trainer as part of the race analysis process. Fortunately each trainer has his/her own approach to training and placing horses. Some trainers, for example, would not consider running a horse if they believed it to be slightly below full fitness, whilst others often run partially fit animals to "leave something to work on". Why this latter approach is accepted by the Jockey Club is a mystery, and though the lack of fitness of some horses is often apparent after the race, the availability of pre-race body-weights of the runners would, for the older horses at least, provide a good guide to their level of fitness. In the meantime this assessment can only be achieved through an analysis of the trainer's historical record or an inspection of the horse in the paddock.

Many trainers have fixed patterns for running horses. Some will always run their best juvenile at a specific course or even in a particular race. An analysis of these trends can be very lucrative. In the Trainer Form column I covered for *Raceform On Saturday*, these trends were referred to as Trainer Pointers and constituted the majority of the column. They would take the form of horses from certain stables running in particular race grades or at particular courses. However, not all trainer trends are positive. Negative trends, such as trainers with very poor success rate with horses running under specific conditions can be just as useful to the punter as the positive trends.

Naturally when considering trainer trends it is necessary to define sets of conditions relating to the horses and races for which the trainer statistics will be of most use. Naturally there is an infinite number of combinations, but the vast majority will not be particularly informative. From research, the key areas for this analysis relate to track and race type, and fitness, previous experience and age of the horse. The following tables detail these critical variables.

Trainer Trends

Trainers often have favourite race courses. Jeremy Tree always took his best two-year-old filly to Newbury for her debut run. Such winners included Interval, Magic Of Life and Stellaria. Others tend to have better success rates with a certain type of horse. This may be a handicap sprinter, or a long distance steeplechaser. The following tables illustrate the success rates for National Hunt trainers by racecourse and race type and is restricted to trainers with profitable recent records form at least 20 runners during the five seasons to end 2003.

National Hunt Trainer Trends – Course and Race Grade

Conditions Hurdle Races

Track	Trainer	Wins	Runs	%	Average Return/£1
Ascot	M C Pipe	8	24	33	+£1.30
Cheltenham	F Doumen	4	10	40	+£0.74
Cheltenham	Miss V Williams	4	12	33	+£0.29

Novices' Hurdle Races

Track	Trainer	Wins	Runs	%	Average Return/£1
Aintree	P J Hobbs	4	13	31	+£1.73
Ascot	M C Pipe	8	22	36	+£0.44
Ascot	M Pitman	5	17	29	+£1.59
Ascot	N J Henderson	8	29	28	+£0.85
Ayr	G M Moore	5	20	25	+£0.84
Bangor	P R Webber	6	21	29	+£0.48
Cheltenham	M Pitman	5	10	50	+£5.85
Cheltenham	P F Nicholls	7	28	25	+£0.27
Doncaster	N J Henderson	5	12	42	+£0.58
Fakenham	Miss V Williams	4	12	33	+£0.51
Folkestone	M Pitman	8	20	40	+£0.72
Folkestone	P J Hobbs	5	10	50	+£0.52
Fontwell	G L Moore	14	55	26	+£0.21
Fontwell	Mrs A J Perrett	4	10	40	+£0.48
Haydock	Mrs S J Smith	8	32	25	+£1.40
Hereford	A King	6	19	32	+£0.42
Hereford	H D Daly	6	22	27	+£0.24
Hereford	N J Henderson	8	17	47	+£1.61
Huntingdon	C R Egerton	5	10	50	+£0.76
Huntingdon	J J O'Neill	4	15	27	+£0.98
Huntingdon	P J Hobbs	6	14	43	+£1.53
Kelso	L Lungo	12	46	26	+£0.60
Ludlow	M C Pipe	11	24	46	+£0.72
Market Rasen	S Gollings	5	19	26	+£0.26
Musselburgh	F Murphy	8	28	29	+£0.32

Novices' Hurdle Races

Track	Trainer	Wins	Runs	%	Average Return/£1
Newton Abbot	I Williams	4	10	40	+£0.31
Perth	J J O'Neill	7	22	32	+£0.30
Perth	L Lungo	9	32	28	+£0.22
Perth	Mrs M Reveley	7	18	39	+£0.21
Plumpton	M C Pipe	22	59	37	+£0.20
Plumpton	N T Chance	4	12	33	+£2.65
Plumpton	P J Hobbs	5	14	36	+£0.66
Plumpton	R H Alner	5	18	28	+£1.65
Sandown	M C Pipe	10	15	67	+£0.34
Stratford	J J O'Neill	9	22	41	+£0.55
Stratford	N J Henderson	4	13	31	+£0.44
Towcester	Miss V Williams	6	18	33	+£0.27
Uttoxeter	M Pitman	5	14	36	+£0.32
Warwick	J J O'Neill	5	17	29	+£1.30
Wetherby	Miss V Williams	4	10	40	+£0.19
Wetherby	N J Henderson	4	11	36	+£0.60
Wincanton	N J Henderson	7	21	33	+£0.20
Worcester	C J Mann	10	18	56	+£1.60
Worcester	J L Spearing	4	14	29	+£3.64
Worcester	Miss V Williams	8	23	35	+£1.01

Selling Hurdle Races

Track	Trainer	Wins	Runs	%	Average Return/£1
Fontwell	M C Pipe	7	14	50	+£0.78
Leicester	M C Pipe	5	11	46	+£0.24
Stratford	M C Pipe	6	17	35	+£0.25

Handicap Hurdle Races

Track	Trainer	Wins	Runs	%	Average Return/£1
Bangor	J J O'Neill	10	36	28	+£0.57
Carlisle	Mrs M Reveley	9	31	29	+£0.31
Carlisle	P Monteith	5	16	31	+£0.29
Catterick	T D Easterby	5	15	33	+£1.26
Cheltenham	P F Nicholls	5	20	25	+£1.52
Chepstow	Miss V Williams	4	15	27	+£0.41
Doncaster	J J O'Neill	7	18	39	+£1.32
Exeter	Mrs S D Williams	4	16	25	+£1.31
Exeter	R J Hodges	7	20	35	+£2.51
Fakenham	F Murphy	4	13	31	+£0.65
Fakenham	H Alexander	4	12	33	+£5.17
Fakenham	N B Mason	5	12	42	+£1.08
Folkestone	B J Llewellyn	4	10	40	+£0.95
Folkestone	R Rowe	4	13	31	+£0.90
Fontwell	Miss V Williams	4	12	33	+£0.30
Fontwell	P F Nicholls	6	15	40	+£0.24
Haydock	J J O'Neill	13	40	33	+£0.24
Haydock	N G Richards	5	15	33	+£0.86
Haydock	S A Brookshaw	4	14	29	+£3.93
Hereford	Miss H C Knight	6	10	60	+£7.13
Hereford	P G Murphy	5	18	28	+£0.25
Hereford	T R George	6	16	38	+£2.13
Hexham	J m Jefferson	4	15	27	+£1.22
Hexham	L Lungo	14	50	28	+£0.27
Hexham	N G Richards	5	12	42	+£0.74
Huntingdon	I Williams	10	39	26	+£0.84
Huntingdon	N J Henderson	6	15	40	+£0.60
Kempton	J J O'Neill	5	13	39	+£0.56
Leicester	J Mackie	7	19	37	+£2.71
Ludlow	M Tate	4	15	27	+£2.65
Market Rasen	Howard Johnson	5	10	50	+£2.05
Market Rasen	I Williams	9	31	29	+£1.49
Market Rasen	J L Spearing	4	15	27	+£1.02
Market Rasen	P Bowen	5	19	26	+£0.47

Handicap Hurdle Races continued

Track	Trainer	Wins	Runs	%	Average Return/£1
Musselburgh	N G Richards	4	10	40	+£1.08
Newton Abbot	A G Hobbs	4	14	29	+£2.04
Perth	N G Richards	6	23	26	+£0.52
Perth	N Twiston-Davies	4	10	40	+£1.97
Sandown	C J Mann	5	19	26	+£0.33
Southwell	B J Llewellyn	5	11	46	+£3.00
Southwell	J R Jenkins	5	19	26	+£0.44
Southwell	Mrs S J Smith	11	39	28	+£0.51
Stratford	P J Hobbs	15	50	30	+£0.70
Warwick	P J Hobbs	5	13	39	+£0.72
Wetherby	J J O'Neill	12	39	31	+£1.25
Worcester	D R Gandolfo	5	17	29	+£0.97
Worcester	R Ford	4	16	25	+£0.97

Conditions Chases

Track	Trainer	Wins	Runs	%	Average Return/£1
Newbury	P F Nicholls	5	11	46	+£0.69
Sandown	P F Nicholls	5	19	26	+£0.27

Handicap Chases

Track	Trainer	Wins	Runs	%	Average Return/£1
Aintree	J J O'Neill	9	21	43	+£1.74
Ascot	M C Pipe	14	47	30	+£0.53
Ayr	Howard Johnson	4	11	36	+£0.67
Bangor	N Twiston-Davies	7	26	27	+£0.39
Carlisle	Mrs M Reveley	5	19	26	+£0.32
Cheltenham	H D Daly	6	22	27	+£1.01
Cheltenham	N J Henderson	12	47	26	+£0.98
Chepstow	P J Hobbs	15	49	31	+£0.45
Doncaster	N B Mason	5	14	36	+£1.70
Exeter	Miss H C Knight	6	23	26	+£0.81
Fakenham	Mrs P Sly	5	17	29	+£0.67
Fakenham	O Brennan	5	11	46	+£2.20
Folkestone	R H Alner	6	22	27	+£0.31
Fontwell	L Wells	5	13	39	+£1.87
Fontwell	P Bowen	5	14	36	+£2.34
Fontwell	P J Hobbs	8	31	26	+£0.55
Haydock	Mrs S J Smith	8	27	30	+£1.74
Haydock	W Jenks	4	12	33	+£0.54
Hereford	S A Brookshaw	4	15	27	+£1.25
Huntingdon	J J O'Neill	5	15	33	+£0.81
Huntingdon	P R Webber	5	15	33	+£0.78
Kelso	N G Richards	4	12	33	+£1.81
Kelso	W Storey	4	13	31	+£0.50
Leicester	P R Webber	4	13	31	+£0.48
Leicester	R Dickin	7	23	30	+£1.59
Ludlow	T R George	6	18	33	+£0.93
Market Rasen	B Ellison	6	16	38	+£2.55
Market Rasen	D L Williams	6	24	25	+£0.20
Market Rasen	M D Hammond	6	24	25	+£0.25
Market Rasen	R C Guest	4	12	33	+£2.52
Musselburgh	L Lungo	6	12	50	+£1.99
Newbury	Miss V Williams	8	23	35	+£0.60
Newbury	N A Gaselee	4	15	27	+£0.62
Newbury	P R Webber	4	15	27	+£0.49

Handicap Chases continued

Track	Trainer	Wins	Runs	%	Average Return/£1
Newcastle	N B Mason	10	29	35	+£1.19
Newcastle	R Johnson	6	24	25	+£1.37
Newton Abbot	J W Mullins	5	18	28	+£1.47
Perth	J J O'Neill	6	18	33	+£1.18
Perth	L Lungo	5	14	36	+£0.24
Perth	R Ford	4	12	33	+£0.25
Sandown	P F Nicholls	13	52	25	+£0.57
Sedgefield	Howard Johnson	13	38	34	+£0.39
Sedgefield	L Lungo	6	19	32	+£1.25
Stratford	P J Hobbs	15	48	31	+£0.67
Taunton	K Bishop	5	18	28	+£1.28
Taunton	M C Pipe	7	22	32	+£0.68
Taunton	Miss V Williams	5	18	28	+£0.56
Towcester	H D Daly	7	25	28	+£0.45
Towcester	Miss V Williams	9	21	43	+£1.54
Towcester	Mrs S J Smith	4	15	27	+£0.40
Towcester	R H Buckler	7	11	64	+£2.04
Uttoxeter	F Murphy	5	15	33	+£1.31
Uttoxeter	J J O'Neill	9	34	27	+£0.38
Uttoxeter	T R George	10	33	30	+£0.69
Wetherby	C Grant	6	13	46	+£1.98
Wetherby	M D Hammond	6	21	29	+£1.49
Wetherby	Mrs M Reveley	20	74	27	+£0.45
Wincanton	A King	4	12	33	+£1.75
Wincanton	N J Hawke	4	15	27	+£1.47
Wincanton	P F Nicholls	27	93	29	+£0.45
Worcester	A G Hobbs	4	14	29	+£0.98
Worcester	P Bowen	10	32	31	+£0.45
Worcester	P F Nicholls	9	29	31	+£0.38

Novices' Chases

Track	Trainer	Wins	Runs	%	Average Return/£1
Cheltenham	J J O'Neill	4	14	29	+£1.44
Cheltenham	N J Henderson	4	12	33	+£0.74
Chepstow	P F Nicholls	14	33	42	+£0.27
Doncaster	Mrs M Reveley	4	11	36	+£2.22
Exeter	P J Hobbs	13	38	34	+£0.29
Fontwell	G L Moore	5	18	28	+£0.60
Fontwell	P F Nicholls	20	45	44	+£0.62
Fontwell	R Rowe	5	20	25	+£1.53
Haydock	Miss V Williams	8	11	73	+£0.87
Hexham	N G Richards	5	12	42	+£0.35
Kempton	N J Henderson	16	29	55	+£0.53
Kempton	R H Alner	4	14	29	+£1.00
Ludlow	P J Hobbs	9	18	50	+£0.36
Market Rasen	D L Williams	4	12	33	+£0.73
Musselburgh	F Murphy	4	13	31	+£0.33
Newbury	N J Henderson	5	11	46	+£0.65
Plumpton	M C Pipe	10	19	53	+£0.20
Sedgefield	B Ellison	8	23	35	+£1.88
Sedgefield	M Todhunter	4	13	31	+£1.08
Stratford	J J O'Neill	4	10	40	+£0.99
Taunton	C Tizzard	4	14	29	+£0.23
Taunton	P F Nicholls	11	24	46	+£0.40
Uttoxeter	M C Pipe	9	16	56	+£0.43
Uttoxeter	P F Nicholls	6	12	50	+£0.23
Uttoxeter	P J Hobbs	5	10	50	+£0.42
Warwick	P F Nicholls	7	15	47	+£0.21
Warwick	P R Webber	4	13	31	+£0.25
Warwick	R Dickin	5	12	42	+£4.43
Wetherby	P Beaumont	4	16	25	+£0.89
Worcester	P Bowen	4	12	33	+£0.85

National Hunt Flat Races

Track	Trainer	Wins	Runs	%	Average Return/£1
Ayr	N G Richards	4	12	33	+£1.44
Carlisle	F Murphy	4	13	31	+£1.04
Carlisle	J J O'Neill	5	12	42	+£0.50
Chepstow	M C Pipe	4	13	31	+£0.23
Chepstow	P F Nicholls	5	15	33	+£0.71
Huntingdon	M Pitman	6	14	43	+£0.74
Huntingdon	N J Henderson	5	19	26	+£0.18
Kempton	N J Henderson	5	15	33	+£0.79
Ludlow	N J Henderson	5	15	33	+£0.28
Ludlow	P R Webber	4	15	27	+£0.35
Market Rasen	M W Easterby	9	21	43	+£0.61
Musselburgh	Mrs M Reveley	4	15	27	+£0.98
Wincanton	P F Nicholls	4	10	40	+£0.18
Wincanton	P J Hobbs	5	15	33	+£1.17
Worcester	P F Nicholls	4	10	40	+£1.92

Race grade key: Novices' Hurdles – non-handicap novices' and maiden hurdle races; Selling Hurdles – non-handicap selling hurdle races; Conditions Hurdles – non-handicap conditions races over hurdles; Handicap Hurdles – all handicap hurdle races (including novices' races); Novices' Chases – non-handicap novices' chases; Conditions Chases – non-handicap conditions chases; Handicap Chases – all handicap chases (including novices' races). The average return is calculated on a level £1 staked at SP. Therefore a return of 0.09 would be required to cover the old off-course tax rate at 9%.

From the National Hunt table it is clear that some trainers favour certain courses. Paul Nicholls, for instance, seems to dominate racing at Chepstow whilst Mary Reveley has good records for many of the northern jumps tracks.

The following table is the Flat Racing equivalent and covers the five years to end 2003

Flat Race Trainer Trends – Course and Race Grade

Juvenile Maiden Races

Track	Trainer	Wins	Runs	%	Average Return/£1
Ayr	B W Hills	8	21	38.1	+£0.44
Ayr	M Johnston	19	55	34.5	+£0.54
Beverley	Sir Mark Prescott	4	15	26.7	+£0.45
Catterick	P F I Cole	5	11	45.5	+£0.73
Doncaster	M A Jarvis	4	13	30.8	+£0.37
Folkestone	P W Harris	4	15	26.7	+£0.38
Hamilton	M R Channon	5	14	35.7	+£0.53
Haydock	J L Dunlop	7	18	38.9	+£0.39
Haydock	M R Channon	7	23	30.4	+£1.26
Leicester	Mrs A J Perrett	5	19	26.3	+£0.41
Leicester	Sir M R Stoute	14	51	27.5	+£0.28
Lingfield (AW)	T G Mills	6	17	35.3	+£0.99
Musselburgh	G A Butler	5	11	45.5	+£0.67
Nottingham	H R A Cecil	6	12	50.0	+£1.58
Pontefract	B W Hills	6	19	31.6	+£0.25
Pontefract	P W Harris	4	13	30.8	+£0.58
Pontefract	W J Haggas	5	13	38.5	+£1.03
Redcar	J H M Gosden	4	11	36.4	+£0.55
Redcar	M R Channon	5	15	33.3	+£0.26
Salisbury	B W Hills	5	20	25.0	+£0.72
Southwell (AW)	J G Given	5	17	29.4	+£0.95
Southwell (AW)	T D Barron	8	26	30.8	+£0.52
Thirsk	M R Channon	5	12	41.7	+£1.00
Wolves. (AW)	B J Meehan	4	16	25.0	+£0.23
Wolves. (AW)	R Hannon	5	19	26.3	+£0.37
Yarmouth	Sir M R Stoute	7	24	29.2	+£0.28
York	D R Loder	4	10	40.0	+£0.38

Juvenile Stakes Races

Track	Trainer	Wins	Runs	%	Average Return/£1
Ayr	M Johnston	4	11	36.4	+£0.57
Doncaster	B A McMahon	5	16	31.3	+£1.72
Doncaster	B W Hills	7	26	26.9	+£1.71
Kempton	R Hannon	5	15	33.3	+£0.31
Lingfield (AW)	G A Butler	6	12	50.0	+£2.52
Lingfield (AW)	R Hannon	8	25	32.0	+£0.37
Lingfield (Turf)	R Hannon	6	12	50.0	+£1.50
Yarmouth	M L W Bell	5	10	50.0	+£1.35

Nursery races

Track	Trainer	Wins	Runs	%	Average Return/£1
Ascot	R Hannon	4	11	36.4	+£1.18
Ripon	T D Easterby	5	15	33.3	+£0.80

Juvenile Listed Races

Track	Trainer	Wins	Runs	%	Average Return/£1
Newbury	M R Channon	4	13	30.8	+£0.18

Non-Juvenile Claiming Races

Track	Trainer	Wins	Runs	%	Average Return/£1
Lingfield (AW)	C N Allen	5	16	31.3	+£0.20
Lingfield (AW)	G L Moore	16	54	29.6	+£0.60
Lingfield (AW)	S C Williams	4	13	30.8	+£0.44
Lingfield (AW)	T G Mills	8	13	61.5	+£1.37
Redcar	D Nicholls	5	13	38.5	+£0.31
Southwell (AW)	T D Barron	12	48	25.0	+£0.19
Wolves. (AW)	A P Jarvis	4	12	33.3	+£0.21
Wolves. (AW)	T D Barron	11	28	39.3	+£0.59

Non-Juvenile Listed Races

Track	Trainer	Wins	Runs	%	Average Return/£1
Ascot	Sir M R Stoute	5	20	25.0	+£0.59
Doncaster	B W Hills	5	12	41.7	+£1.68
Doncaster	M Johnston	4	12	33.3	+£1.35
Goodwood	G Wragg	6	20	30.0	+£0.83
Goodwood	H R A Cecil	4	11	36.4	+£0.51
Goodwood	M P Tregoning	4	10	40.0	+£1.63
Kempton	J L Dunlop	8	18	44.4	+£1.02
Newbury	J L Dunlop	4	14	28.6	+£0.27
Newbury	M Johnston	4	12	33.3	+£0.86
Newmarket	M P Tregoning	9	20	45.0	+£0.58

Non-Juvenile Group Races

Track	Trainer	Wins	Runs	%	Average Return/£1
Ascot	M Johnston	9	33	27.3	+£1.10
Ascot	M P Tregoning	5	17	29.4	+£0.85
Goodwood	M P Tregoning	4	10	40.0	+£1.95
Goodwood	Saeed Bin Suroor	4	10	40.0	+£0.48
Newbury	J L Dunlop	5	16	31.3	+£0.69
York	Saeed Bin Suroor	5	15	33.3	+£0.75

Non-Juvenile Maiden Races

Track	Trainer	Wins	Runs	%	Average Return/£1
Ayr	B W Hills	6	14	42.9	+£0.60
Bath	Mrs A J Perrett	7	24	29.2	+£0.37
Bath	Sir M R Stoute	7	23	30.4	+£0.31
Beverley	J R Fanshawe	4	12	33.3	+£0.24
Beverley	Sir M R Stoute	6	11	54.5	+£0.33
Chepstow	H Candy	4	14	28.6	+£0.54
Chepstow	J L Dunlop	6	14	42.9	+£0.99
Doncaster	B W Hills	12	42	28.6	+£0.66
Doncaster	H R A Cecil	5	19	26.3	+£1.22
Folkestone	Mrs A J Perrett	7	10	70.0	+£0.47
Goodwood	J H M Gosden	15	46	32.6	+£0.45
Haydock	B W Hills	7	28	25.0	+£1.45
Haydock	L M Cumani	4	12	33.3	+£0.55
Haydock	Sir M R Stoute	10	28	35.7	+£0.32
Kempton	E A L Dunlop	4	12	33.3	+£0.74
Lingfield (AW)	J H M Gosden	7	25	28.0	+£0.89
Lingfield (AW)	J Noseda	12	39	30.8	+£0.23
Lingfield (AW)	M A Jarvis	5	14	35.7	+£2.63
Lingfield (AW)	T G Mills	6	23	26.1	+£0.72
Lingfield (Turf)	J L Dunlop	5	19	26.3	+£0.20
Lingfield (Turf)	J Noseda	4	12	33.3	+£1.67
Lingfield (Turf)	M P Tregoning	5	12	41.7	+£0.59
Lingfield (Turf)	Sir M R Stoute	8	16	50.0	+£0.62
Musselburgh	M Johnston	6	14	42.9	+£0.65
Newbury	Mrs A J Perrett	4	14	28.6	+£1.46
Newcastle	M R Channon	8	10	80.0	+£1.60
Newmarket	D R C Elsworth	7	22	31.8	+£0.95
Newmarket	J H M Gosden	15	60	25.0	+£0.30
Nottingham	A C Stewart	4	12	33.3	+£0.45
Nottingham	J H M Gosden	7	25	28.0	+£0.19
Nottingham	J R Fanshawe	5	14	35.7	+£0.38
Pontefract	A C Stewart	5	17	29.4	+£0.62
Pontefract	B W Hills	6	21	28.6	+£0.40

Non-Juvenile Maiden Races continued

Track	Trainer	Wins	Runs	%	Average Return/£1
Pontefract	L M Cumani	5	18	27.8	+£0.26
Pontefract	M A Jarvis	4	16	25.0	+£0.54
Pontefract	Sir M R Stoute	9	29	31.0	+£0.23
Redcar	J Noseda	6	10	60.0	+£1.86
Ripon	B W Hills	15	30	50.0	+£0.94
Ripon	H R A Cecil	7	13	53.8	+£0.49
Sandown	Sir M R Stoute	9	34	26.5	+£0.42
Southwell (AW)	M Johnston	7	18	38.9	+£1.00
Thirsk	B W Hills	6	12	50.0	+£0.82
Thirsk	H R A Cecil	8	14	57.1	+£0.27
Thirsk	J L Dunlop	7	10	70.0	+£1.22
Thirsk	Sir M R Stoute	6	22	27.3	+£0.48
Warwick	Sir M R Stoute	7	15	46.7	+£0.61
Windsor	R Charlton	5	19	26.3	+£0.44
Windsor	Sir M R Stoute	22	60	36.7	+£0.38
Wolves. (AW)	A P Jarvis	4	15	26.7	+£0.19
Wolves. (AW)	J Noseda	7	17	41.2	+£0.76
Wolves. (AW)	M L W Bell	5	17	29.4	+£0.22
Wolves. (AW)	W J Haggas	12	25	48.0	+£0.58
Yarmouth	M A Jarvis	4	10	40.0	+£0.67
York	Sir M R Stoute	6	10	60.0	+£0.46

Non-Juvenile Stakes Races

Track	Trainer	Wins	Runs	%	Average Return/£1
Ascot	Sir M R Stoute	6	11	54.5	+£0.49
Ayr	A Bailey	5	13	38.5	+£1.04
Beverley	T D Easterby	5	13	38.5	+£1.17
Brighton	M R Channon	7	17	41.2	+£1.96
Doncaster	P F I Cole	5	17	29.4	+£0.33
Doncaster	R Hannon	4	12	33.3	+£0.61
Haydock	T D Easterby	4	12	33.3	+£0.40
Kempton	Mrs A J Perrett	5	11	45.5	+£0.55
Leicester	M L W Bell	4	13	30.8	+£2.66
Lingfield (AW)	D J S Cosgrove	4	10	40.0	+£2.20
Lingfield (AW)	G A Butler	7	25	28.0	+£0.53
Lingfield (AW)	M Johnston	5	16	31.3	+£0.32
Lingfield (AW)	M R Channon	5	15	33.3	+£1.13
Newbury	J L Dunlop	5	13	38.5	+£1.03
Newmarket	J R Fanshawe	6	24	25.0	+£0.40
Newmarket	M Johnston	4	14	28.6	+£0.34
Newmarket	Mrs A J Perrett	8	14	57.1	+£2.22
Ripon	M Johnston	6	12	50.0	+£1.96
Southwell (AW)	B A McMahon	5	16	31.3	+£1.03
Wolves. (AW)	D J S Cosgrove	4	15	26.7	+£1.53
Wolves. (AW)	T D Barron	6	16	37.5	+£0.86
Yarmouth	B Hanbury	4	12	33.3	+£0.27
Yarmouth	J L Dunlop	7	10	70.0	+£0.80

Non-Juvenile Handicaps

Track	Trainer	Wins	Runs	%	Average Return/£1
Ayr	A Turnell	4	16	25.0	+£2.69
Ayr	W J Haggas	8	18	44.4	+£0.92
Beverley	J L Dunlop	8	24	33.3	+£0.25
Beverley	L M Cumani	4	10	40.0	+£1.30
Brighton	C F Wall	7	23	30.4	+£1.81
Brighton	E A L Dunlop	7	20	35.0	+£0.43
Brighton	G A Butler	7	24	29.2	+£1.36
Brighton	P A Blockley	5	10	50.0	+£2.15
Brighton	Sir Mark Prescott	8	21	38.1	+£0.22
Catterick	A Turnell	4	13	30.8	+£0.71
Catterick	Sir Mark Prescott	4	11	36.4	+£0.27
Chepstow	E A L Dunlop	4	13	30.8	+£1.04
Chepstow	M C Pipe	5	18	27.8	+£1.14
Chester	J L Dunlop	5	15	33.3	+£0.41
Chester	P F I Cole	9	28	32.1	+£0.67
Doncaster	J R Fanshawe	5	19	26.3	+£0.32
Epsom	H Morrison	5	10	50.0	+£1.81
Epsom	S C Williams	5	17	29.4	+£1.12
Goodwood	J G Given	4	12	33.3	+£3.04
Hamilton	G L Moore	4	13	30.8	+£1.73
Haydock	G A Butler	6	21	28.6	+£0.75
Haydock	M A Jarvis	9	26	34.6	+£1.29
Haydock	Sir Mark Prescott	6	16	37.5	+£0.73
Kempton	M C Pipe	6	14	42.9	+£1.23
Kempton	T G Mills	9	35	25.7	+£1.33
Leicester	J L Dunlop	13	45	28.9	+£0.73
Leicester	P F I Cole	7	26	26.9	+£0.39
Lingfield (AW)	A Turnell	4	16	25.0	+£1.25
Lingfield (AW)	C F Wall	11	38	28.9	+£0.55
Lingfield (AW)	Sir Mark Prescott	10	28	35.7	+£0.71
Lingfield (Turf)	C F Wall	6	18	33.3	+£2.25
Lingfield (Turf)	D Nicholls	5	15	33.3	+£0.90
Lingfield (Turf)	M L W Bell	4	13	30.8	+£0.65
Musselburgh	M L W Bell	4	12	33.3	+£0.73

Non-Juvenile Handicaps continued

Track	Trainer	Wins	Runs	%	Average Return/£1
Musselburgh	Sir Mark Prescott	7	13	53.8	+£1.74
Musselburgh	T D Easterby	10	38	26.3	+£0.46
Newbury	J R Fanshawe	5	20	25.0	+£0.34
Newcastle	W J Haggas	7	21	33.3	+£0.52
Nottingham	J H M Gosden	4	12	33.3	+£1.63
Nottingham	J R Fanshawe	4	15	26.7	+£0.52
Nottingham	Sir Mark Prescott	5	18	27.8	+£0.23
Salisbury	R Charlton	8	27	29.6	+£0.64
Sandown	A C Stewart	11	30	36.7	+£1.16
Sandown	M P Tregoning	4	12	33.3	+£0.90
Sandown	P F I Cole	7	26	26.9	+£1.49
Sandown	S C Williams	5	17	29.4	+£2.79
Southwell (AW)	H Morrison	11	31	35.5	+£1.46
Thirsk	J L Dunlop	4	11	36.4	+£0.55
Thirsk	J R Fanshawe	4	10	40.0	+£0.77
Warwick	H Morrison	5	13	38.5	+£2.28
Warwick	J L Dunlop	5	12	41.7	+£0.61
Warwick	M Johnston	5	19	26.3	+£0.19
Windsor	M Johnston	5	17	29.4	+£1.54
Windsor	T G Mills	7	26	26.9	+£0.68
Wolves. (AW)	M A Jarvis	12	37	32.4	+£0.92
Wolves. (AW)	T G Mills	10	37	27.0	+£0.89
York	Mrs A J Perrett	4	14	28.6	+£1.45

Race grade key: Juvenile races are those races restricted to horses aged two-years-old. Non-Juvenile races are races for horses aged three-years and older (including races restricted to three-year-olds only). Group races include Group 1, 2 and 3 events. The average return is calculated on a level £1 staked at SP. Therefore a return of 0.09 would be required to cover the old off-course tax rate at 9%.

Though the track-race type classification is a useful pointer there are more interesting statistics when the profile of the horse is also considered.

The majority of horses will, at some point in their racing careers, race in a handicap. And whilst some trainers have better records in these races than others, as evidenced by the previous two tables, an analysis of the trainer's record with horses making their handicap debut is even more interesting.

For many National Hunt horses this first handicap run is encountered twice: in hurdle races and in chases, and these two events need to be analysed separately. The following table details the record for horses having their first run in a handicap hurdle race and covers just those trainers which have had a sufficient number of qualifiers to make the statistics reliable.

Handicap Hurdle Races

Trainer	All Race Win Rate	First Run Win Rate	First Run Average Return/£1
T R George	17.7%	22.2%	+£1.10
L Lungo	18.0%	18.3%	-£0.16
P F Nicholls	18.2%	18.3%	-£0.19
T D Easterby	10.9%	17.5%	+£0.06
M C Pipie	15.3%	17.4%	-£0.07
Mrs M Reveley	15.2%	17.2%	-£0.01
A W Carroll	10.2%	16.7%	+£0.58
N J Henderson	13.4%	16.1%	+£0.04
J M Jefferson	11.2%	15.2%	+£0.26
A King	13.1%	14.3%	+£0.01
P J Hobbs	15.3%	14.2%	-£0.08
J J O'Neill	18.9%	13.8%	-£0.42
R T Phillips	13.0%	12.5%	-£0.43
I Williams	15.2%	11.7%	-£0.18
R H Alner	10.9%	11.6%	-£0.13
Miss V Williams	14.2%	11.4%	-£0.32
Howard Johnson	15.3%	11.4%	-£0.48
Mrs S J Smith	13.6%	11.3%	-£0.18
H D Daly	8.7%	11.1%	-£0.12
C J Mann	13.1%	10.0%	-£0.59
M D Hammond	8.3%	10.0%	-£0.38
G M Moore	13.1%	9.8%	-£0.17
B J Llewellyn	8.8%	9.5%	+£0.19
M Pitman	11.0%	9.3%	-£0.38
N Twiston-Davies	11.9%	9.0%	-£0.38
O Sherwood	9.8%	8.5%	-£0.42
F Murphy	9.1%	7.9%	-£0.60
G L Moore	11.7%	7.4%	-£0.49
M W Easterby	15.0%	7.3%	-£0.54

Handicap Hurdle Races continued

Trainer	All Race Win Rate	First Run Win Rate	First Run Average Return/£1
G B Balding	8.8%	7.1%	-£0.58
J A B Old	9.7%	6.4%	-£0.68
N Meade	6.5%	6.0%	-£0.54
P Bowen	11.7%	5.9%	-£0.69
K C Bailey	10.3%	5.1%	-£0.69
P R Webber	9.9%	5.0%	-£0.64
Miss H C Knight	11.7%	4.2%	-£0.68
R Rowe	10.8%	4.2%	-£0.85
R H Buckler	5.3%	3.9%	-£0.65
K A Morgan	9.8%	2.5%	-£0.89
R Dickin	9.1%	2.2%	-£0.76
N B Mason	11.7%	1.9%	-£0.94
P J Rothwell	6.6%	1.3%	-£0.86
E McNamara	6.3%	0.0%	-£1.00
S J Mahon	1.8%	0.0%	-£1.00

The average return refers to horses making their debut in a handicap hurdle race.

The first numeric column shows the success rate for each trainer for all runners in handicap hurdle races. The First Run column details the success rate for just those horses making their handicap hurdle debut and the final column shows the average return for a level £1 staked on all first handicap run horses. The equivalent table for handicap chasers is given next, the format remains the same as for the previous table.

Handicap Chases

Trainer	All Race Win Rate	First Run Win Rate	First Run Average Return/£1
P F Nicholls	19.5%	30.1%	+£0.12
L Lungo	21.7%	25.6%	+£0.23
R H Alner	15.1%	23.5%	+£0.53
P J Hobbs	16.9%	23.3%	+£0.23
Miss H C Knight	13.6%	18.6%	+£0.39
P R Webber	16.1%	18.6%	+£0.72
F Murphy	13.3%	18.2%	+£0.07
Mrs M Reveley	17.2%	17.9%	-£0.26
N J Henderson	17.6%	17.7%	-£0.12
I Williams	16.2%	17.3%	+£0.28
Mrs S J Smith	17.3%	17.0%	+£0.05
N Meade	11.6%	16.7%	-£0.10
H D Daly	17.3%	15.6%	+£0.00
R Dickin	13.6%	15.4%	+£0.43
Miss V Williams	17.3%	15.0%	-£0.26
M C Pipe	13.4%	13.9%	-£0.34
K C Bailey	12.3%	13.9%	+£0.16
J J O'Neill	15.7%	13.4%	-£0.02
R H Buckler	12.9%	13.3%	+£1.97
T R George	15.5%	13.0%	+£0.41
O Sherwood	7.4%	12.2%	-£0.52
A King	12.3%	12.1%	+£0.22
N Twiston-Davies	11.9%	11.8%	+£0.02
D McCain	6.9%	9.4%	-£0.17
P Bowen	18.0%	9.1%	-£0.44
R Rowe	10.2%	8.9%	+£0.10
Howard Johnson	12.8%	8.6%	-£0.50
N B Mason	15.3%	8.6%	-£0.65
M D Hammond	13.5%	8.5%	-£0.28

The average return refers to horses making their debut in a handicap chase.

With these horses the important factor is the comparison between the success rates for all handicappers and those making their handicap debuts. For instance Norman Mason has a good success rate with his handicap chasers, but those running in handicap company for the first time have a very poor record. Whilst these ratios are similar for many trainers there are some that excel with their handicappers. For example, Tim Easterby has a success rate with handicap hurdle debut runners which is almost twice his overall success rate. From this statistic it could be concluded that Easterby knows the ability of his horses and is able to exploit a lenient handicap mark. On the other hand it may be suggested that Easterby is adept at qualifying his potential handicappers without exposing their true level of ability resulting in these horses receiving a handicap rating that does not reflect their capabilities.

Trainers at the other end of the table either use this first run to gauge the ability of their horses against proven handicap runners, or are simply unable to exploit the handicapping system because the animals they train do not, in general, possess a great deal of ability. There is more scope for winning handicaps if a trainer is able to make a good horse appear to be no more than average. However, if the horse is only average to start with the possibility of receiving a winning handicap rating is extremely slim.

Other interesting features relate to the return column. Richard Rowe has a poorer success rate with handicap chase debutants, however, backing each one would have produced a level stake profit. Some trainers have excellent return figures for their runners, which indicates that these horses are under bet by the public and consequently are worth close examination. Such information can be used to formulate systems or to support the traditional methods of form study.

Similar tables can be generated for Flat racing with two-year-old handicaps (nurseries) analysed separately from non-juvenile races. These tables are given next.

Nursery Races

Trainer	All Race Win Rate	First Nursery Run Win Rate	First Run Average Return/£1
Sir Mark Prescott	26%	23%	+£0.46
P W Harris	13%	19%	+£0.67
R M Beckett	15%	19%	+£0.75
P F I Cole	18%	18%	+£0.42
M L W Bell	13%	17%	+£0.29
A P Jarvis	8%	16%	+£0.26
N A Callaghan	19%	16%	-£0.07
C E Brittain	11%	15%	+£0.87
J L Dunlop	12%	15%	-£0.26
B A McMahon	11%	14%	-£0.22
T D Barron	12%	13%	-£0.22
M Johnston	11%	13%	-£0.29
A Bailey	9%	12%	-£0.06
B W Hills	14%	11%	-£0.50
R Hannon	9%	11%	-£0.18
M Blanshard	6%	10%	+£1.15
P C Haslam	11%	10%	-£0.59
N P Littmoden	12%	10%	+£0.05
B J Meehan	9%	10%	-£0.17
T D Easterby	10%	9%	-£0.40
J S Moore	8%	8%	-£0.10
R F Johnson Houghton	11%	8%	-£0.71
B R Millman	6%	8%	-£0.45
E A L Dunlop	10%	8%	-£0.06
J A Osborne	19%	8%	-£0.57
B Smart	11%	7%	-£0.41
J G Given	8%	7%	+£0.01
M W Easterby	7%	7%	-£0.08
M R Channon	10%	7%	-£0.38
A Berry	5%	6%	-£0.49
M H Tompkins	6%	5%	-£0.64
K A Ryan	6%	5%	-£0.60
N Tinkler	7%	4%	-£0.75
Mrs P N Dutfield	1%	3%	-£0.70
P D Evans	8%	3%	-£0.67
R A Fahey	4%	0%	-£1.00
Miss L A Perratt	3%	0%	-£1.00

The average return refers to horses making their debut in a handicap races.

A few trainers have a better success rate with their nursery runners which are making their debut in handicap company and these should be noted carefully. The following table presents the same data for non-juvenile races. The First Run column refers to horses having their first handicap run, consequently these horses will not have raced in nurseries.

Non-Juvenile Handicap Races

Trainer	All Race Win Rate	First NurseryRun Win Rate	First Run Average Return/£1
Sir Mark Prescott	27.6%	27.0%	-£0.19
G A Butler	15.9%	20.7%	+£0.36
J R Fanshawe	16.9%	16.8%	-£0.07
L M Cumani	14.4%	16.7%	+£0.03
P F I Cole	12.5%	16.4%	+£0.34
M C Pipe	10.6%	16.3%	+£0.15
Sir M R Stoute	14.1%	15.5%	-£0.06
J Noseda	13.0%	14.8%	-£0.09
T G Mills	14.2%	14.6%	+£0.21
M Johnston	13.2%	14.3%	+£0.12
T D Barron	10.2%	13.9%	+£0.10
W J Haggas	14.1%	13.9%	-£0.23
Bob Jones	10.1%	13.9%	+£0.71
E A L Dunlop	12.6%	13.6%	-£0.08
R Charlton	14.5%	13.6%	-£0.17
M A Jarvis	14.1%	13.6%	-£0.22
R M H Cowell	11.9%	13.2%	+£0.06
A C Stewart	16.5%	13.1%	-£0.17
J L Dunlop	14.8%	13.0%	-£0.27
J H M Gosden	12.6%	13.0%	-£0.15
H Morrison	11.8%	12.7%	+£0.08
W Jarvis	10.0%	12.5%	+£0.27
C F Wall	12.1%	12.4%	-£0.11
Andrew Reid	7.7%	12.4%	+£0.16
P W Hiatt	11.9%	11.9%	+£0.23
S Gollings	8.6%	11.8%	-£0.07
J G Given	9.3%	11.6%	-£0.01
Miss B Sanders	7.3%	11.5%	-£0.05
R A Fahey	10.4%	11.3%	-£0.13

Non-Juvenile Handicap Races continued

Trainer	All Race Win Rate	First NurseryRun Win Rate	First Run Average Return/£1
D W Barker	8.3%	11.2%	+£0.07
J Balding	10.1%	11.2%	-£0.25
G L Moore	9.1%	11.1%	-£0.05
P C Haslam	13.3%	11.0%	+£0.08
M L W Bell	9.9%	10.8%	+£0.03
P J Makin	10.9%	10.5%	+£0.09
D Nicholls	8.2%	10.4%	-£0.13
S C Williams	9.5%	10.4%	-£0.20
P W Harris	8.6%	10.3%	-£0.04
J L Spearing	9.2%	10.3%	-£0.02
N P Littmoden	9.2%	10.2%	-£0.08
J A R Toller	9.2%	10.2%	+£0.05
B R Millman	7.1%	10.0%	+£0.02
C N Allen	7.2%	10.0%	-£0.09
D R C Elsworth	9.6%	9.9%	-£0.06
I A Wood	9.4%	9.9%	-£0.23
W M Brisbourne	9.8%	9.8%	-£0.11
A G Newcombe	8.3%	9.6%	-£0.20
J A Osborne	8.3%	9.5%	-£0.35
Miss Gay Kelleway	7.8%	9.4%	-£0.23
Mrs M Reveley	9.7%	9.3%	-£0.44
W Storey	6.6%	9.3%	-£0.35
H Candy	8.1%	9.3%	-£0.32
K R Burke	7.7%	9.2%	-£0.09
I Semple	8.9%	9.2%	+£0.10
G M Moore	6.7%	9.1%	+£0.00
C G Cox	6.8%	9.0%	-£0.06
J Akehurst	8.1%	8.9%	-£0.19
P D Evans	7.7%	8.8%	-£0.21
Mrs A J Perrett	10.2%	8.8%	-£0.33
J A Glover	9.9%	8.8%	-£0.15
J M P Eustace	8.1%	8.7%	-£0.16
M R Channon	8.3%	8.6%	-£0.28
J J Quinn	8.0%	8.6%	-£0.32

Non-Juvenile Handicap Races continued

Trainer	All Race Win Rate	First NurseryRun Win Rate	First Run Average Return/£1
G C Bravery	8.2%	8.6%	-£0.32
R M Whitaker	6.9%	8.6%	-£0.05
W R Muir	7.4%	8.5%	-£0.15
E A Wheeler	9.5%	8.4%	-£0.25
K A Ryan	7.8%	8.3%	-£0.04
S Kirk	7.1%	8.3%	-£0.17
W J Musson	9.0%	8.2%	-£0.22
R Hollinshead	6.5%	8.1%	-£0.12
Lady Herries	6.0%	8.0%	-£0.29
B Ellison	8.9%	7.9%	-£0.39
B Hanbury	9.0%	7.8%	-£0.28
M W Easterby	9.4%	7.7%	-£0.24
J Hetherton	6.4%	7.4%	-£0.23
P S Felgate	6.8%	7.3%	-£0.38
R Hannon	7.3%	7.2%	-£0.44
M Blanshard	4.6%	7.2%	-£0.26
J W Payne	7.3%	7.2%	-£0.37
J M Bradley	6.8%	7.1%	-£0.46
B W Hills	8.4%	7.0%	-£0.46
J W Hills	6.9%	7.0%	-£0.15
M C Chapman	5.2%	7.0%	-£0.31
A P Jarvis	6.4%	7.0%	-£0.21
R J Hodges	7.5%	7.0%	-£0.42
N Tinkler	6.2%	6.9%	-£0.37
C A Dwyer	6.0%	6.9%	-£0.15
Mrs N MacCauley	6.1%	6.8%	-£0.36
P Howling	3.9%	6.8%	-£0.34
B J Meehan	7.3%	6.7%	-£0.37
J S Goldie	7.6%	6.6%	-£0.52
M Dods	6.3%	6.5%	-£0.20
D W Chapman	6.1%	6.4%	-£0.36
A Bailey	6.2%	6.4%	-£0.50
JB Smart	8.7%	6.3%	-£0.11
M D I Usher	7.0%	6.2%	-£0.31

Non-Juvenile Handicap Races continued

Trainer	All Race Win Rate	First NurseryRun Win Rate	First Run Average Return/£1
R Brotherton	7.1%	6.2%	-£0.55
C E Brittain	7.7%	6.1%	-£0.45
B Palling	4.3%	6.1%	-£0.30
R M Beckett	5.6%	6.1%	-£0.13
A M Balding	8.4%	5.9%	-£0.69
Jedd O'Keeffe	4.1%	5.9%	-£0.27
D Shaw	5.8%	5.8%	-£0.43
Miss L A Perratt	5.1%	5.8%	-£0.26
M H Tompkins	6.9%	5.6%	-£0.08
J R Jenkins	8.1%	5.5%	-£0.57
S Dow	5.4%	5.3%	-£0.55
M J Polglase	5.3%	5.3%	-£0.58
T D Easterby	7.8%	5.1%	-£0.44
Ian Williams	4.6%	4.9%	-£0.22
H J Collingridge	7.5%	4.8%	-£0.51
N A Callaghan	9.3%	4.6%	-£0.52
M Brittain	5.2%	4.5%	-£0.23
P Monteith	5.0%	4.2%	-£0.73
A Berry	4.3%	4.1%	-£0.62
C N Kellett	3.6%	3.5%	-£0.34
J J Bridger	3.7%	2.9%	-£0.43
Mrs S Lamyman	5.0%	2.8%	-£0.64
B A McMahon	6.2%	2.6%	-£0.76
Mrs J R Ramsden	7.1%	2.5%	-£0.82
Mrs P N Dutfield	2.0%	1.8%	-£0.79
A W Carroll	4.8%	1.8%	-£0.82

The average return refers to horses making their debut in a handicap races.

Horses returning for a long layoff are often ignored by punters, especially in Jump races. The reasons for this are quite clear. Many of these horses will not be anywhere near peak fitness and as such are very unlikely to win. However, there are some trainers who are able to get their horses ready for a run at home and often these horses start at inflated prices, providing the bettor with an edge. The following table shows the performance of horses returning from a break of at least 100 days for Jump races.

All Jumps Races

Trainer	Win Rate with all Horses	Win Rate for Horses running after a break of at least 100 days	Average Return/ £1 Staked
P F Nicholls	25.0%	26.2%	+£0.08
N J Henderson	21.9%	25.0%	+£0.17
Miss V Williams	20.1%	20.4%	-£0.17
M C Pipe	21.6%	20.2%	-£0.06
Noel Chance	18.1%	20.0%	-£0.22
P J Hobbs	20.3%	19.5%	-£0.09
N G Richards	19.8%	18.9%	+£0.23
R H Alner	13.2%	18.7%	+£0.18
P Monteith	11.7%	17.9%	+£0.84
J J O'Neill	19.3%	17.9%	-£0.16
O Sherwood	13.7%	17.3%	-£0.28
Mrs M Reveley	17.3%	16.8%	-£0.21
Miss H C Knight	15.9%	16.7%	-£0.22
H D Daly	14.5%	15.9%	+£0.11
G L Moore	12.4%	15.2%	-£0.18
L Lungo	20.6%	15.2%	-£0.45
M W Easterby	14.6%	14.6%	-£0.16
M Pitman	14.5%	14.5%	-£0.25
N Twiston-Davies	12.9%	14.4%	-£0.31
I Williams	14.9%	14.3%	-£0.01
Mrs S J Smith	13.7%	14.0%	+£0.27
S E H Sherwood	15.8%	14.0%	-£0.37
P R Webber	14.2%	13.0%	-£0.08
J M Jefferson	12.3%	12.9%	+£0.09
J Mackie	11.4%	12.7%	-£0.06
C J Mann	15.0%	12.6%	+£0.39
A King	15.2%	12.3%	-£0.17
J A B Old	9.7%	12.2%	-£0.17
N Meade	15.1%	12.1%	-£0.37
Howard Johnson	12.0%	11.8%	-£0.21
T R George	14.1%	11.8%	-£0.21
F Murphy	13.6%	11.3%	-£0.43
R Dickin	10.2%	11.3%	+£0.30

All Jumps Races continued

Trainer	Win Rate with all Horses	Win Rate for Horses running after a break of at least 100 days	Average Return/ £1 Staked
R Rowe	9.2%	11.0%	+£0.05
A Streeter	8.9%	10.7%	+£0.16
R T Phillips	15.0%	10.3%	-£0.32
K C Bailey	11.9%	10.0%	-£0.26
G M Moore	12.6%	9.9%	-£0.43
P Bowen	14.4%	9.9%	-£0.32
R H Buckler	8.0%	9.8%	+£0.10
R Lee	11.2%	9.6%	-£0.34
D R Gandolfo	10.4%	9.5%	-£0.20
D J Wintle	11.1%	8.5%	-£0.50
M D Hammond	12.4%	8.2%	-£0.37
T D Easterby	14.4%	7.7%	-£0.47
D McCain	6.2%	7.6%	-£0.35
N B Mason	11.4%	7.2%	-£0.66
B G Powell	9.3%	7.1%	-£0.43
R J Hodges	8.7%	6.2%	-£0.54
G B Balding	6.9%	6.1%	-£0.19
C Grant	8.9%	5.6%	-£0.53
J Neville	5.8%	3.8%	-£0.79
P J Rothwell	6.7%	3.8%	-£0.57
R G Frost	8.3%	3.4%	-£0.70
P Beaumont	9.3%	2.8%	-£0.86

The average return refers to horses running after a break of least 100 days.

From the previous table it can be seen that the success rate for horses returning from a break can differ markedly from the trainer's overall win ratio. For some trainers this ratio can be less than half their all-horse average. Clearly these are horses to avoid. However, there are a few trainers who do better with these runners than the market suggests, and consequently they are worth following. Paul Nicholls, for instance, has an overall success rate of about 25% whereas his win ratio for horses running after a break is over 26%. A level stake bet on each of these at starting price would have yielded a good profit. Possibly the course absence is deterring punters from backing these horses making them value bets for punters with a knowledge of Nicholls' success rate with this type of horse.

When Martin Pipe has a runner that has not been on a course for a considerable length of time, commentators usually remark that the horse "will not want for fitness" and the results given in the table support this statement. Pipe has an overall success rate of 21.6% and the horses returning from a break score at a very similar rate of 20.2%. Robert Alner, on the other hand, does exceptionally well with these horses and based on the data given previously this is a fact that is not fully accounted for in the starting price, and until it is these horses are worth following.

All Flat Races

Trainer	Win Rate with all Horses	Win Rate for Horses running after a break of at least 100 Days	Average Return/ £1 Staked
Sir M R Stoute	21.2%	27.5%	+£0.29
Sir Mark Prescott	27.6%	26.6%	-£0.06
J H M Gosden	18.3%	21.0%	+£0.03
H R A Cecil	19.3%	19.9%	-£0.21
B W Hills	12.5%	17.0%	+£0.01
J L Dunlop	17.0%	16.6%	-£0.11
G A Butler	15.6%	16.3%	+£0.10
T G Mills	15.1%	15.9%	+£0.41
M P Tregoning	20.8%	15.4%	-£0.15
M Johnston	15.7%	15.2%	+£0.07
E A L Dunlop	14.3%	14.9%	-£0.16
M A Jarvis	16.3%	14.9%	+£0.38
W J Haggas	17.2%	14.5%	-£0.17
J R Fanshawe	16.7%	14.1%	-£0.32
L M Cumani	16.3%	14.1%	-£0.23
R Charlton	17.0%	14.1%	-£0.29
Mrs A J Perrett	14.5%	14.0%	+£0.02
G Wragg	14.6%	13.3%	-£0.17
M L W Bell	11.5%	13.0%	+£0.00
J W Hills	8.6%	10.6%	-£0.07
M C Pipe	12.6%	10.2%	-£0.24
P F I Cole	13.1%	9.7%	-£0.29
P J Makin	11.3%	9.7%	-£0.08
J Noseda	17.0%	9.5%	-£0.11
T D Barron	12.5%	9.0%	-£0.34
B J Meehan	9.3%	8.9%	-£0.28
D R C Elsworth	11.2%	8.9%	-£0.04
B Smart	10.1%	8.8%	+£0.62
C E Brittain	8.2%	8.6%	-£0.25

All Flat Races continued

Trainer	Win Rate with all Horses	Win Rate for Horses running after a break of at least 100 Days	Average Return/ £1 Staked
P W Harris	8.8%	7.8%	-£0.22
P C Haslam	14.3%	7.8%	-£0.33
B A McMahon	7.4%	7.7%	-£0.02
J R Jenkins	7.4%	7.6%	-£0.07
A P Jarvis	8.1%	7.4%	-£0.28
M H Tompkins	8.4%	6.3%	-£0.39
C F Wall	11.5%	6.3%	-£0.66
Mrs M Reveley	10.5%	6.1%	-£0.62
R Hannon	8.9%	5.7%	-£0.62
K A Ryan	8.8%	5.7%	-£0.37
J G Given	9.5%	5.4%	-£0.36
M R Channon	9.9%	5.2%	-£0.67
G L Moore	10.0%	5.2%	-£0.46
W M Brisbourne	9.3%	4.8%	-£0.28
R A Fahey	10.8%	4.7%	-£0.58
M Dods	6.3%	4.6%	-£0.25
B Palling	5.0%	4.5%	-£0.13
B R Millman	7.9%	4.4%	-£0.51
W R Muir	7.6%	4.3%	-£0.38
K R Burke	9.1%	4.2%	-£0.74
T D Eaasterby	8.5%	4.0%	-£0.62
D Shaw	6.2%	4.0%	-£0.72
J S Goldie	7.3%	3.9%	-£0.11
R Hollinshead	6.9%	3.7%	-£0.36
M W Easterby	9.0%	3.6%	-£0.52
A Berry	4.9%	3.5%	-£0.33
S Dow	6.2%	3.1%	-£0.76
M Brittain	4.8%	3.1%	-£0.35
N P Littmoden	9.5%	2.8%	-£0.58
M Blanshard	5.8%	2.8%	-£0.44
P D Evans	7.7%	2.7%	-£0.56
N Tinkler	6.2%	2.3%	-£0.78
Miss L A Perratt	5.2%	2.2%	-£0.14
J J Quinn	9.1%	2.0%	-£0.72
D Nicholls	9.2%	1.8%	-£0.86
A Bailey	6.1%	1.7%	-£0.87
J M Bradley	6.5%	1.0%	-£0.84
J S Wainwright	4.1%	0.9%	-£0.86

CHAPTER 2
UTILISING RECENT STABLE FORM

References to a trainer's current level of form are made daily in the racing press or on television. And whilst this is a crucial factor to consider, the accuracy of the assessment is equally as critical. For instance it is not unusual to hear a commentator state that a particular stable is in good form simply following a single winner. Whilst this may be true, it is a very bold statement to make based on one race. In fact there is evidence to support this claim. During the 2000/01 National Hunt season the success rates of horses from yards where a stablemate had won the previous race was 15%, this compared to 11% for those runners following a stable loser. Though this is a remarkable statistic it does not imply the stable is in form, more information than a single winner is required to make an accurate assessment of this key element of race analysis.

Analysing Recent Form

The Racing Post lists daily the success rates for every trainer during the last fourteen days. Essentially the table shows the number of winners, placed horses and losers for each stable as well as the number of days and runs since a winner. Given this information and the fact that stables have higher success rates following winners than following losers, an analysis of the recent wins to runs ratio is a good starting point for assessing a stable's current level of form.

Figure 1: 20-race rolling average for a Jumps Trainer through a single season

The graph given in Figure 1 shows the success rate for a top National Hunt trainer through the 2000/01 Jumps season based on a rolling 20-runner sample. To calculate a point on the graph the number of winners in a sample of twenty consecutive runners is counted and divided by the sample size; to locate the next point, the first result in the sample is removed and the next race performance added and the number of winners, and averages, recalculated. Apparently it was a roller-coaster season for the handler, but in fact this type of graph is typical for most trainers. With peaks of over 50% and lows near zero, it is clear that an assessment of the recent form of a handler can provide the bettor with valuable information. For instance, would you like to be backing this trainer's horses during the periods where he achieved a success rate of at best 1 in 20?

But is there any statistical evidence, apart from this graph, to suggest that a trainer's recent form is a guide to his/her future form? During the 2000/01 Jumps season trainers with a run of 20 consecutive losers won 145 races with their next runner, but this was from a total of 2051 attempts, giving a success rate of just 7% and a level stake loss at starting price of 30p/£1. For those with one winner in the last 20, the success rate of the next horse rose slightly to 8% but again a heavy betting loss would have been incurred. In fact it was not until the recent success rate reached 40% (i.e. eight winners from the last twenty runners) that a positive betting return was achieved on the following bet. The overall loss, though, was reduced to a more respectable level of 11p/£1 once the recent success ratio reached 25%.

Whilst this ratio is an interesting statistic, it hides important information. For instance a recent success ratio for a stable of 25% may be considered a positive factor for placing a bet. However, from the graph it can be seen that the (central) peak reaches a value of 55% and that the 25% ratio is crossed on either side of this high point. On the incline side the trainer's horses are improving his strike rate as the ratio progresses towards the peak. On the downside the 25% ratio is achieved by consecutive losers reducing the formerly high figure. A one-in-four success rate equates to five winners from twenty runners.

Series of Race Results for a Trainer	Average Success Rate
W L L W W L W L L W L L L L L L L L L L	25%
L L L L L L W L L L L L W L L W W W L L	25%
20th race .... latest race	

As the trainer's success rate improves these five winners are very likely to be found towards the end of the sample representing the most recent runners, thus accounting for the gradual improvement in the ratio. For the downslope these winners would have be recorded at the opposite end of the sample, in fact for a 25% success rate it would be possible for the trainer to be on a losing run of 15. Clearly it is better to be following a trainer as his/her success rate improves than following a trainer who is experiencing a decline in his/her fortune following a peak. For our top Jumps trainer graphed in Figure 1 following his horses after a success rate of 25% or higher would have produced a profit of 58 points to a level £1 stake throughout the season. However, reducing the bets to periods when his/her success rate was increasing resulted in a return of 79 points, with bets when the ratio was declining returning a loss of 21 points. Though this is not an exact science, since it is not known in advance whether a maximum has been reached, it is possible to get a good idea of how the trainer's success rate is likely to move from a graph similar to that given here. And given the level of profit achieved in the example, calculating this success ratio could be a very profitable move.

Improving the Recent Form Measure

Whilst this simple approach works well for assessing a trainer's current level of form, with the use of a computer it is possible to develop methods that are a little more complex in structure, but which provide a more complete assessment. The three main areas for further development are as follows: the method for assessing individual race performances (at present a victory indicates a good run and a defeat a poor run); calculating the optimal value for the size of the sample on which the trainer's assessment is based; and the inclusion of a time variable.

The key question is: When is a stable in form? As with most questions of this type it is easy to give comparatively extreme examples to answer this query. For instance, a trainer who has a success rate of over 90% with his last 30 runners could be considered to have his horses running well, similarly a trainer with no winners from the last 30 runners would be assumed to be out of form. Though these examples are easy to classify in terms of a trainer's current form, they represent the extremes of the possible range of examples and in-between there is a huge grey area packed with examples that are not as easily classified.

Like so many solutions to real-life problems, the simplest way to represent the form of a stable is numerically. The rolling 20-runner success ratio provides an easily interpreted scale against which to assess the form of the trainer. By definition the resulting figure can take one of 21 possible values determined by the most recent racecourse performances. Consequently this scale provides sufficient detail on which the form assessments can be made. The lowest value this ratio can take is zero representing no winners from the last twenty runs. The highest value is 100 representing 20 winners, with the scale calibrated in 5% bands. An analysis of this scale can then be used to categorise the trainer's level of form. In an earlier example a value of 25% was used as a threshold to indicate good form, though this figure is not fixed and should be re-evaluated periodically. But is 20 the ideal sample size from which to calculate the ratio?

The optimal sample size on which to base the rolling average is not easy to determine. A small value will be unreliable and unstable, whereas a large sample size will merely converge to the trainer's overall average success rate (see graph given in Figure 2). The sample size needs to be sufficiently large to result in a stable distribution without losing the variability produced by the trainer's changes in fortune. Given these conditions it is entirely possible that the optimum figure would vary depending on the number of runners a trainer has during certain times of the year. One method that could be used to find the optimal value would employ a genetic algorithm. However, such an analysis is beyond the scope of this article. Personally I have found twenty to be the best figure though I have no doubt that other sample sizes will work as well, and possibly better.

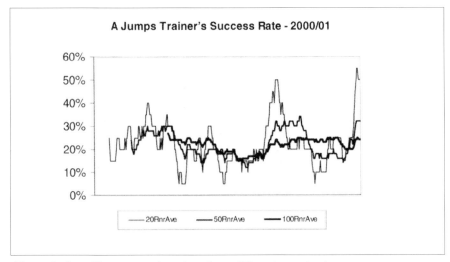

Figure 2: the rolling average based on three different sample sizes

Including a Time Index

Earlier it was found that a profit could be achieved when the 20-runner rolling average reached a certain point and that this profit improved significantly if the trainer's recent success rate was increasing. Under such circumstances the majority of winners in the sample would have been recorded most recently, whereas for declining success ratios these recent runners are in most cases losers which results in the decrease in the ratio. Clearly this indicates that as well as the sample size the time factor covering the sample is also important.

Naturally, when assessing the recent form of a horse, jockey or trainer, the latest races are the most important, so the inclusion of a time variable in our trainer form assessment is a relatively obvious step. The simplest approach is to index the races included in the sample and incorporate this index into the calculation of the Trainer Form Figure. Fixing this index is somewhat arbitrary and different methods can be employed, but the simplest way is to set the index for the latest performance to 1, then increment the value for each previous race performance down to a value of 20 for the final race in the sample. Calculating the Trainer Form Figure (TFF) is then a case of summing the individual race figures derived by the following formula for each of the 20 races in the sample:

individual race figure = result/(1+index), where result is 1 for a win, zero for a defeat
Trainer Form Figure (TFF) = sum of all twenty individual race figures

This formula places greatest emphasis on the most recent race. If the trainer won with his latest runner the value of this race figure is 1/(1+1) or 0.5, a winner with the 20th runner generates a value of 1/(20+1) or approximately 0.05. A loser generates an individual race figure of zero which does not increase the TFF. Using these formulae generates a single value for the TFF ranging from zero (no winners in the 20-runner sample) to 2.65 (all 20 runners won). Normalising this to a scale of 0 to 100 is straightforward, simply divide the TFF by 2.65 then multiply by 100.

Applying this method to our top trainer then analysing the profit/loss against the TFF values produced some interesting results. Following the trainer's horses when the TFF was low returned a significant loss, however, for TFF values over 25 a significant profit was produced, 35p for every £1 staked at starting price.

Though this method works well there is a slight weakness which can be removed with a more complex approach. The index weights each race performance in a fixed manner without taking into account the time differences between the races. For instance, a trainer may not have had a runner for several months yet the index scale does not change with respect to this absence. Instead the last runner's performance would be weighted the same as if the horse had run only two days previously. Under these conditions the TFF should tend to a value indicating that it is not possible to determine the level of recent form. In other words the formula should be structured in such a way that it is apparent from the TFF that reliably assessing whether the stable is in form or not is not possible from the data available.

The simplest solution is to limit the sample of races to a predefined time span, such as one month. Consequently only runners that have run within the last 31 days would be considered for inclusion in the sample. However, this may result in the sample containing fewer than the minimum number of race performances, and an adjustment would need to be made to the normalising procedure to correct the TFF. And having fewer than the optimum number of race performances in the sample would also weaken the final result. Alternatively the index in the previous formula could be replaced by a stricter time variable such as the number of days since the race giving the following formula:

individual race figure = result/(1+number of days since race)

With this approach the most recent performances would still have the greatest influence on the TFF. For example a winner the previous day would add 1/(1+1), or 0.5, to the TFF, whereas a winner 40 days ago would add only 1/(1+40) or 0.02.

Naturally the TFF does not need to be used in its current form. Users may find that it places too much emphasis on the latest runners in which case increasing the "1" in the denominator to some higher figure such as 10 would reduce their impact. Again some form of optimising method could be used to generate the most effective scale. For instance the formula may be rewritten as:

individual race figure = result/(10+number of days since race)

As the constant in the denominator increases the influence of the most recent race performances diminishes.

Redefining a Good Run

So far the analysis has been based on the wins to runs ratio and has not accounted for horses that have run well without winning. Under this "winners only" approach a horse beaten a short-head in a 25-runner race could impact negatively on the trainer's success ratio with a short-head winner of a two-horse race adding positively to the trainer's ratio. Clearly such an approach can be improved upon. In Forecasting Methods For Horseracing (Raceform, 1998; High Stakes 2002) I discussed this issue and concluded that a "good" performance can be determined from the following rule:

> if distance beaten in pounds <= starting price
> then performance is good

Such a rule uses the starting price as a guide to where the horse should finish in the race and then compares this to the animal's actual distance beaten (converted to pounds using the standard scale). So using this rule a horse starting at 3-1 would be considered to have run well if it was beaten less than three lengths in a jumps race and one length in a five furlong sprint. The TFF formula can then be amended with the race assessment replacing the result.

Summary

This article has attempted to illustrate the importance of recent stable form in race analysis and has proposed several different approaches for assessing this factor. The suggested methods have varied in complexity, some are straightforward to calculate but the approaches probably require the use of a computer. Whilst the article merely scratches the surface of this interesting topic it is clear from the findings that even a very simplistic approach can have a positive impact of the performance of a series of bets. And with a little further work, better, simpler, methods could no doubt be developed. It is certainly worth considering especially given the profits that could result.

CHAPTER 3
TRAINERS, JOCKEYS AND OWNERS

Though trainer-jockey combinations are a popular selection method for punters, a third factor which has an influence on the performance of this approach, and can easily be added, is the owner. Trainers' success rates vary significantly when analysed with respect to the owner. This is for a variety of reasons, but predominantly because some owners simply buy better horses than others which is reflected in the trainer's record.

With three key variables there are, naturally, three approaches to the analysis. Firstly, the trainer's runners can be isolated and then analysed with respect to jockey and owner; secondly the jockey's mounts can be sampled and analysed by trainer and owner; and finally the owners horses can be examined by jockey and trainer. Each approach is valid, and though there will be a considerable amount of overlap between the three sets of results, such an approach can help to identify profitable combinations previously unconsidered.

Trainer Analysis – Sir Michael Stoute

Due to the relatively small samples associated with trainer-based information, it is easy to "over analyse" the data in order to generate impressive results based on only a few races. Consequently it is better to adopt a more general approach to the data with very few sub-classifications. In the following analyses the races are subdivided by age: juvenile and non-juvenile; and race type: handicap and non-handicap. Such an approach preserves the samples to more meaningful sizes.

Table 1 presents a list of the performances of Sir Michael Stoute's two-year-olds for a selection of his main owners.

Table 1: Sir Michael Stoute's Two-Year-Olds Sub-Divided by Owner

Owner	Wins	Runs	Success Rate (%)	Average Return/£1
Cheveley Park Stud	16	63	25.4%	-£0.22
H H Aga Khan	5	31	16.1%	-£0.59
Hamdan Al Maktoum	9	26	34.6%	+£0.56
K Abdulla	5	23	21.7%	-£0.30
Lord Weinstock	1	11	9.1%	-£0.80
Maktoum Al Maktoum	4	15	26.7%	+£0.50
Niarchos Family	4	13	30.8%	-£0.21
Saeed Suhail	5	27	18.5%	+£0.44
Sheikh Mohammed	2	11	18.2%	+£0.41
The Queen	3	16	18.8%	-£0.53

Though the samples are small, it is easy to see the owners for whom Sir Michael Stoute has the best results. In terms of profit, horses owned by Hamdan Al Maktoum are the ones to follow. Table 2 covers the older horses and due to the increased sample sizes is more informative.

Table 2: Sir Michael Stoute's Non-Juvenile Runners Sub-Divided by Owner

Non-Juvenile Runners	Non-Handicaps				Handicaps			
Owner	Wins	Runs	Success Rate (%)	Average Return/£1	Wins	Runs	Success Rate (%)	Average Return/£1
Cheveley Park Stud	23	75	30.7%	+£0.41	4	41	9.8%	-£0.58
H H Aga Khan	38	154	24.7%	-£0.19	6	48	12.5%	-£0.57
Hamdan Al Maktoum	10	47	21.3%	+£0.28	1	14	7.1%	-£0.73
Highclere Thoroughbred Racing Ltd	9	29	21.0%	-£0.04	1	11	9.1%	+£0.36
Lord Weinstock	16	49	32.7%	+£0.35	2	17	11.8%	+£0.00
Maktoum Al Maktoum	7	35	20.0%	-£0.25	2	9	22.2%	-£0.07
Saeed Suhail	8	35	22.9%	-£0.19	1	11	9.1%	-£0.70
Sheikh Mohammed	9	22	40.9%	+£0.99	3	11	27.3%	+£0.68
The Queen	4	28	14.3%	-£0.75	2	17	11.8%	-£0.65

Based on the results given in Table 2, Stoute is worth following when he runs a horse owned by Cheveley Park Stud, Hamdan Al Maktoum, Lord Weinstock or Sheikh Mohammed in a non-handicap. His success rate with these runners is reasonable, and the level stake profit at starting price makes interesting reading.

A jockey-based analysis can also prove to be profitable. Table 3 shows the success rate for Sir Michael Stoute's juvenile horses by jockey, and Table 4 presents the same analysis for non-juvenile runners.

Table 3: Sir Michael Stoute's Two-Year-Olds Sub-Divided by Jockey

Jockey	Wins	Runs	Success Rate (%)	Average Return/£1
F Lynch	15	49	30.6%	+£0.45
J P Murtagh	7	30	23.3%	+£0.50
K Fallon	18	83	21.7%	-£0.40
Pat Eddery	3	26	11.5%	-£0.60
R Hills	9	22	40.9%	+£0.63

Table 4: Sir Michael Stoute's Non-Juveniles Sub-Divided by Jockey

Non-Juvenile Runners	Non-Handicaps				Handicaps			
Owner	Wins	Runs	Success Rate (%)	Average Return/£1	Wins	Runs	Success Rate (%)	Average Return/£1
F Lynch	30	88	34.1%	-£0.10	2	35	5.7%	-£0.84
J Fortune	4	17	23.5%	+£1.94	1	3	33.3%	+£0.08
J P Murtagh	9	42	21.4%	+£0.15	2	19	10.5%	+£0.05
K Fallon	64	254	25.2%	-£0.05	12	87	13.8%	-£0.22
Pat Eddery	19	68	27.9%	-£0.17	4	26	15.4%	-£0.42
R Hills	5	34	14.7%	-£0.65	1	12	8.3%	-£0.69
R Hughes	2	18	11.1%	-£0.73	3	17	17.6%	-£0.25

Though Kieren Fallon has ridden the most winners for Stoute, his success rate is far lower than that achieved by other jockeys and a level stake bet on all mounts would have returned a considerable loss. This is only to be expected since the price of Fallon-ridden horses will be reduced simply due to the jockey and even though Fallon is the best jockey on the Flat at present his additional ability is more than compensated for by the price reduction, making his horses a poorer betting medium. Fergal Lynch and Richard Hills are the jockeys to follow on Michael Stoute's juveniles, whilst for the older horses there is little to be gained by following any specific rider.

Owner Analysis – Cheveley Park Stud

Alternatively it is possible to take an owner and analyse by jockey and trainer to generate another set of profitable combinations. For instance Cheveley Park Stud have many horses in training with Michael Stoute. However, they also use several other trainers and analyses of their results for juvenile and non-juvenile horses is given in Tables 5 and 6.

Table 5: Cheveley Park Stud Two-Year-Old Runners Analysed by Trainer

Trainer	Wins	Runs	Success Rate (%)	Average Return/£1
E A L Dunlop	0	2	0.0%	-£1.00
J R Fanshawe	4	18	22.2%	+£0.22
M A Jarvis	0	1	0.0%	-£1.00
M L W Bell	6	28	21.4%	-£0.39
Mrs A J Perrett	4	11	36.4%	+£0.75
Sir Mark Prescott	7	29	24.1%	+£0.65
Sir Michael Stoute	16	63	25.4%	-£0.22
W J Haggas	2	21	9.5%	-£0.75

Table 6: Cheveley Park Stud Non-Juvenile Runners Analysed by Trainer

Non-Juvenile Runners			Non-Handicaps			Handicaps		
Owner	Wins	Runs	Success Rate (%)	Average Return/£1	Wins	Runs	Success Rate (%)	Average Return/£1
E A L Dunlop	0	1	0.0%	-£1.00	-	-	-	-
J R Fanshawe	6	34	17.6%	-£0.38	5	24	20.8%	+£0.51
M L W Bell	1	12	8.3%	-£0.81	0	2	0.0%	-£1.00
Mrs A J Perrett	5	11	45.5%	+£2.93	1	6	16.7%	-£0.54
Sir Mark Prescott	6	19	31.6%	+£0.59	3	14	21.4%	-£0.39
Sir Michael Stoute	23	75	30.7%	+£0.41	4	41	9.8%	-£0.58
W J Haggas	10	26	38.5%	+£1.18	2	17	11.8%	-£0.64

Clearly Michael Stoute trains the highest proportion of Cheveley Park Stud horses, but with respect to the juveniles Sir Mark Prescott is the trainer to follow, along with Amanda Perrett and James Fanshawe. Of the older horses, James Fanshawe's runners in handicaps should be noted as well as those from Perrett stable in non-handicaps.

Table 7: Cheveley Park Stud Two-Year-Old Runners Analysed by Jockey

Jockey	Wins	Runs	Success Rate (%)	Average Return/£1
G Duffield	2	15	13.3%	-£0.33
K Fallon	9	26	34.6%	-£0.17
M Fenton	3	14	21.4%	-£0.27
Pat Eddery	1	16	6.3%	-£0.84
S Sanders	6	19	31.6%	+£0.57

Table 8: Cheveley Park Stud Non-Juvenile Runners Analysed by Jockey

Non-Juvenile Runners			Non-Handicaps			Handicaps		
Owner	Wins	Runs	Success Rate (%)	Average Return/£1	Wins	Runs	Success Rate (%)	Average Return/£1
F Lynch	7	15	46.7%	+£0.30	0	4	0.0%	-£1.00
G Duffield	1	11	9.1%	-£0.81	2	7	28.6%	-£0.05
K Fallon	14	42	33.3%	+£0.01	4	29	13.8%	-£0.64
M Hills	4	10	40.0%	+£1.71	0	4	0.0%	-£1.00
O Urbina	1	6	16.7%	-£0.52	1	4	25.0%	+£0.63
Pat Eddery	5	12	41.7%	+£0.28	0	4	0.0%	-£1.00
S Sanders	7	14	50.0%	+£2.58	1	8	12.5%	-£0.67
T Quinn	2	5	40.0%	+£1.30	1	7	14.3%	-£0.61

From Table 7 it appears that, whilst Fallon has the highest proportion of winning rides for Cheveley Park Stud, his mounts tend to be under-priced resulting in a level stake loss. Seb Sanders, on the other hand, has a similar success rate but also a positive expectation in terms of return. So based on these data it would be more profitable to follow Sanders as opposed to Fallon.

For the older horses, Fallon again rides the most winners, and for non-handicaps at least, returns a slight profit. Seb Sanders is again a good jockey to follow in these events, along with Michael Hills, Pat Eddery and Fergal Lynch.

Jockey Analysis – Kieren Fallon

The final type of analysis concerns jockeys. Analysing the horses ridden by Kieren Fallon with respect to the trainer produces the data presented in Tables 9 and 10.

Table 9: Kieren Fallon's Juvenile Rides Analysed by Trainer

Trainer	Wins	Runs	Success Rate (%)	Average Return/£1
A Bailey	4	11	36.4%	+£0.67
B J Meehan	3	10	30.0%	+£1.73
E A L Dunlop	1	17	5.9%	-£0.92
N A Callaghan	4	13	30.8%	+£0.13
P F I Cole	1	13	7.7%	-£0.75
R Hannon	0	11	0.0%	-£1.00
Sir Michael Stoute	18	83	21.7%	-£0.37
W J Haggas	3	12	25.0%	-£0.28

Table 10: Kieren Fallon's Non-Juvenile Runners Analysed by Trainer

Non-Juvenile Runners	Non-Handicaps			Handicaps			
Owner	Wins	Runs	Success Rate (%)	Average Return/£1	Wins	Runs	Success Rate (%)	Average Return/£1
D Nicholls	5	15	33.3%	-£0.22	5	36	13.9%	-£0.14
D R C Elsworth	0	11	0.0%	-£1.00	3	20	15.0%	+£0.08
E A L Dunlop	4	12	33.3%	-£0.07	4	32	12.5%	-£0.40
G A Butler	3	22	13.6%	-£0.60	10	32	31.3%	+£0.71
J L Dunlop	5	23	21.7%	-£0.16	0	8	0.0%	-£1.00
P F I Cole	1	11	9.1%	-£0.36	2	9	22.2%	+£0.54
Sir Michael Stoute	64	253	25.3%	-£0.05	12	88	13.6%	-£0.23
W J Haggas	4	10	40.0%	+£0.07	2	12	16.7%	-£0.45
W J Musson	0	2	0.0%	-£1.00	4	19	21.1%	-£0.20

A 36.4% success rate for Fallon riding two-year-olds trained by Alan Bailey is interesting and worth noting, likewise the figures for Meehan and Callaghan. But for older horses the Fallon-Butler pairing in handicap races stands out in terms of success rate and profitability and is the best combination to follow.

Table 11: Kieren Fallon's Non-Juvenile Runners Analysed by Owner

Non-Juvenile Runners			Non-Handicaps			Handicaps	
Owner	Wins	Runs	Success Rate (%)	Average Return/£1	Wins	Runs	Success Rate (%)	Average Return/£1
Cheveley Park Stud	14	42	33.3%	+£0.01	4	29	13.8%	-£0.64
D R Brotherton	2	8	25.0%	+£0.56	1	3	33.3%	+£0.25
Erik Penser	0	1	0.0%	-£1.00	4	10	40.0%	+£2.10
H H Aga Khan	13	51	25.4%	-£0.16	2	7	28.6%	+£0.18
Highclere Thoroughbred Racing Ltd	6	21	28.6%	-£0.15	0	9	0.0%	-£1.00
Lord Weinstock	9	21	42.9%	+£0.92	1	5	20.0%	+£1.60
Mrs Denis Haynes	2	9	22.2%	+£0.00	1	4	25.0%	+£0.75
Robert Hitchins	3	11	27.3%	+£1.89	1	15	6.7%	-£0.63
Saeed Suhail	5	17	29.4%	+£0.23	1	7	14.3%	-£0.54
Sheikh Mohammed	5	10	50.0%	+£0.92	1	2	50.0%	+£3.00
The Queen	3	14	21.4%	-£0.62	0	5	0.0%	-£1.00

Fallon's success rates for Lord Weinstock and Sheikh Mohammed in non-handicaps are far superior to the remainder, but essentially there is little in this analysis to form the basis of a system. Clearly this type of analysis is very dependent on trainers retaining jockeys and owners from season to season. So before it is used as part of a system or as part of a computer model it is necessary to ensure riding arrangements have not significantly changed, or that the key owners have not changed their horse placing policies.

The following tables were generated using Raceform Interactive and list a small selection of profitable combinations based on the four years to end 2003 for both Flat and Jumps racing.

Juveniles

Trainer	Jockey	Owner	Race Type	Wins	Runs	Average Return/£1
B W Hills	Any	Maktoum Al Maktoum	Non-Hcp	12	53	£0.62
J H M Gosden	J Fortune	Any	Non-Hcp	33	134	£0.18
J H M Gosden	J Fortune	K Abdulla	Non-Hcp	8	12	£2.14
M Johnston	Any	Paul Dean	Non-Hcp	5	16	£0.90
M Johnston	K Darley	Any	Non-Hcp	41	169	£0.17
M Johnston	R Hills	Any	Non-Hcp	4	8	£1.59

Non-Juveniles

Trainer	Jockey	Owner	Race Type	Wins	Runs	Average Return/£1
Any	K Darley	Maktoum Al Maktoum	Non-Hcp	11	25	£1.38
B W Hills	Any	Maktoum Al Maktoum	Non-Hcp	14	83	£0.19
H Morrison	R Hughes	Any	Hcp	8	46	£0.29
J H M Gosden	R Hills	Hamdan Al Maktoum	Non-Hcp	17	56	£0.73
M Johnston	Any	Maktoum Al Maktoum	Non-Hcp	17	68	£0.19
M Johnston	Any	P D Savill	Non-Hcp	6	16	£2.03
M Johnston	Any	Jaber Abdullah	Hcp	6	13	£1.88
M Johnston	Any	Maktoum Al Maktoum	Hcp	13	56	£0.24
M Johnston	J Fanning	Any	Hcp	46	272	£0.19
M Johnston	K Dalgleish	Any	Hcp	48	308	£0.16
M Johnston	R Hills	Any	Non-Hcp	6	14	£1.72
R Charlton	R Hughes	K Abdulla	Non-Hcp	19	62	£0.28
R Charlton	R Hughes	Any	Hcp	14	63	£0.67

Jumps Races

Trainer	Jockey	Owner	Race Type	Wins	Runs	Average Return/£1
Any	A Dobbin	Ashleybank Invest.	Chases	14	38	£0.33
Any	A Dobbin	J P McManus	Chases	7	20	£0.85
L Lungo	A Dobbin	Any	Chases	39	114	£0.20
L Lungo	W Dowling	Any	Hurdles	17	120	£0.19
L Lungo	Any	Ashleybank Invest.	Hurdles	38	110	£0.22
Mrs S J Smith	Any	Trevor Hemmings	Chases	20	107	£0.28
Mrs S J Smith	D Elsworth	Any	Chases	45	164	£0.55
Mrs S J Smith	J Crowley	Any	Chases	15	71	£0.57
Mrs S J Smith	W Marston	Any	Chases	17	92	£0.33
Mrs S J Smith	S Durack	Any	Hurdles	13	68	£0.57
Mrs S J Smith	W Marston	Any	Hurdles	20	97	£0.45
Mrs S J Smith	Any	Trevor Hemmings	Hurdles	13	72	£0.65
P Bowen	R Johnson	Any	Chases	11	25	£0.71
P F Nicholls	S Stronge	Any	Chases	12	45	£0.19
P F Nicholls	Any	C G Roach	Chases	14	41	£0.29
P F Nicholls	Any	R M Penny	Chases	12	35	£0.15
P F Nicholls	A Honeyball	Any	Hurdles	9	27	£2.11
P F Nicholls	Any	C G Roach	Hurdles	20	56	£0.32
P F Nicholls	R Walsh	Any	Hurdles	34	127	£0.22
P J Hobbs	A P McCoy	Any	Chases	15	39	£0.29
P J Hobbs	Any	The Country Side	Chases	10	35	£0.55
P J Hobbs	Any	Mrs Karola Vann	Hurdles	10	29	£0.65
P J Hobbs	Any	R J B Partners	Hurdles	16	36	£1.25
P J Hobbs	R Johnson	Peter Emery	Hurdles	4	5	£1.56
R T Phillips	R Johnson	Any	Chases	12	33	£0.27

CHAPTER 4
WIN AND EACH WAY BETTING

As the price of a selection increases the bettor's thoughts tend to turn to the each way option. The reason for this is quite clear. Longer priced horses are less likely to win and hence a win bet is less likely to return a profit. So in order to increase the chance of a positive return the bettor opts for an each way bet. This is a reasonable approach especially if the bettor's aim is to generate regular short-term profits. However, from a strict profit perspective, is each way betting preferable to the straight win approach?

The Theoretical Argument

There is a theoretical argument that makes it clear that each way betting is not as profitable as win betting. Consider a five horse race with each of the runners starting at 4/1. Putting £2.00 to win on each horse returns £10.00, the same as the total outlay. Staking £1 each way on the five runners incurs the same £10.00 outlay as for the win bets; however, the return is different. Using the current each way fraction of one-quarter of the odds the return is given as follows:

From the winner:	£1 at 4/1 and £1 at evens.	Return £7
From the second:	£1 at evens.	Return £2

The total return from the each way bets is £9.00, which means that a loss has been incurred betting each way compared to a zero profit from the win bets. The loss is simply due to the each way fraction, which in the above example is one-quarter of the odds. So, what fraction should be used to produce an equivalent return to win betting?

It is possible to calculate the fair each way fractions by considering similar examples to the one given earlier. These fractions are presented in Figures 1 and 2 for non-handicap and handicap races respectively.

From Figure 1, it can be seen that, in non-handicaps, the current fraction of one-fifth for races of 8 or more runners represents very poor value, and as the number of runners increases the gap between the current and fair fraction widens meaning that the each way punter is receiving even poorer value.

For handicaps (Figure 2) the picture is similar, although for races of 16 runners or more the current fraction is acceptable. Clearly, the worst case is a seven runner race when the fair fraction should be about two-fifths, nearly double the current fraction of one-quarter.

Figure 1: Fair each way fractions for non-handicap races

Number of Runners	Current Fraction	Fair Fraction	Places
5	0.25	0.38	1,2
6	0.25	0.40	1,2
7	0.25	0.42	1,2
8	0.20	0.24	1,2,3
9	0.20	0.25	1,2,3
10	0.20	0.26	1,2,3
12	0.20	0.27	1,2,3
14	0.20	0.28	1,2,3
16	0.20	0.29	1,2,3
20	0.20	0.30	1,2,3
25	0.20	0.31	1,2,3

Figure 2: Fair each way fractions for handicap races

Number of Runners	Current Fraction	Fair Fraction	Places
5	0.25	0.38	1,2
6	0.25	0.40	1,2
7	0.25	0.42	1,2
8	0.20	0.24	1,2,3
9	0.20	0.25	1,2,3
10	0.20	0.26	1,2,3
12	0.25	0.27	1,2,3
14	0.25	0.28	1,2,3
16	0.25	0.20	1,2,3,4
20	0.25	0.21	1,2,3,4
25	0.25	0.22	1,2,3,4

Therefore, each way betting seems to offer a poorer option to win only betting, except for handicaps of 16 runners or more where the fraction works in the bettor's favour.

The Practical Experience

Though in theory each way betting offers a poorer betting medium, in practice the outcome is slightly different. Taking a random sample of 4430 Flat races consisting of five or more runners staged during the period 1999-2002 a 1 point win bet placed on each would have returned a loss of 33% (i.e. 33p for every £1 staked), whereas placing ½ point each way bets would have returned a loss of only 28%. This is in direct contrast to the theoretical findings that imply the losses should be greater for the each way bets.

Furthermore, these results are repeated when the analysis is subdivided by field size and race grade as illustrated by Figure 3.

Figure 3: Average return for win and each way bets by field size and race type

	Non-Handicaps		Handicaps		All Races	
Field Size (rns)	Win	EW	Win	EW	Win	EW
5-7	-£0.25	-£0.27	-£0.12	-£0.20	-£0.22	-£0.25
8-11	-£0.32	-£0.25	-£0.22	-£0.22	-£0.28	-£0.24
12-15	-£0.39	-£0.37	-£0.29	-£0.26	-£0.33	-£0.31
16-20	-£0.48	-£0.47	-£0.35	-£0.22	-£0.38	-£0.29
21+	-£0.60	-£0.58	-£0.41	-£0.30	-£0.46	-£0.37
All Races	-£0.37	-£0.34	-£0.30	-£0.24	-£0.33	-£0.28

The advantage of each way betting is greatest in 16-20 runner handicaps, as predicted by the theoretical analysis. From Figure 3 it can be seen that the loss for this particular group is only 22% compared to a win loss of 35%. And apart from the very small field sizes, up to seven runners, the each way return always beats the win return for handicaps and non-handicaps alike. Figure 4 shows the average return by starting price, again each way seems to be the better option.

Figure 4: Average return for win and each way bets by starting price

	Non-Handicaps		Handicaps		All Races	
Field Size (rns)	Win	EW	Win	EW	Win	EW
Odds On	-£0.04	-£0.03	-£0.09	-£0.08	-£0.05	-£0.03
Evens-2/1	-£0.05	-£0.05	-£0.10	-£0.10	-£0.07	-£0.07
85/40-4/1	-£0.11	-£0.10	-£0.10	-£0.11	-£0.11	-£0.11
9/2-5/1	-£0.07	-£0.11	-£0.11	-£0.11	-£0.10	-£0.11
11/2-6/1	-£0.12	-£0.12	-£0.13	-£0.13	-£0.13	-£0.13
13/2-8/1	-£0.15	-£0.15	-£0.19	-£0.14	-£0.17	-£0.14
17/2-10/1	-£0.22	-£0.21	-£0.25	-£0.19	-£0.24	-£0.20
11/1-16/1	-£0.36	-£0.32	-£0.30	-£0.23	-£0.32	-£0.26
18/1-25/1	-£0.44	-£0.40	-£0.39	-£0.31	-£0.41	-£0.34
28/1+	-£0.76	-£0.68	-£0.60	-£0.50	-£0.70	-£0.61
All Prices	-£0.37	-£0.34	-£0.30	-£0.24	-£0.33	-£0.28

It appears each way betting has distinct advantages at almost all prices and for any field size. This is because of the disproportionately high number of placed horses at long prices. From Figure 4 it can be seen that the rates of return are broadly similar for horses near the front of the market, yet the gap begins to widen as the price increases, with the each way loss for horses priced at 28/1 or longer approximately 87% of the win loss. The implication of these findings is that for the longer priced horses the bettor is likely to lose less by adopting the each way approach.

Given that each way betting may offer advantages over win betting under certain circumstances, the next question to consider is whether there is anyway this can be exploited to return a profit to the bettor. In the past, the each way fraction was reduced to 1/6 when the favourite was odds on. Fortunately this is no longer the case so races featuring odds on favourites would appear to be a good starting point for further analysis.

Figure 5: Average return for each way bets placed on the second favourite by price and field size for handicap races featuring an odds on favourite

Price of 2nd		Number of Runners			
Favourite	5-7	8-11	12-15	16-20	All
9/4-10/3	-£0.54	+£0.58	-	-	-£0.24
7/2-5/1	-£0.15	-£0.49	-	-£1.00	-£0.27
11/2-9/1	-£0.36	-£0.20	+£0.50	-£0.63	-£0.22
10/1-22/1	-	-£1.00	-	-	-£1.00
All Prices	-£0.28	-£0.21	+£0.50	-£0.75	-£0.25

Based on Figure 5 the possibility of returning a profit from backing second favourites each way in handicap races where the favourite is odds on looks minimal. Though there is a glimmer of hope in the 8-11 runner category. Second favourites priced in the 9/4–10/3 range in this group return a good looking profit of 58p for every £1 staked. However, the number of qualifiers is so low that this is more likely to be a statistical outlier than a long term trend. This comment also applies to the 12-15 runner category.

The results presented in Figure 6 look more promising given the increased number of plus signs indicating a profitable return.

When the second favourite is priced between evens and 2/1 an each way bet would produce a loss of about 8p for every £1 staked. However, an analysis of this return by field size shows an improving trend as the field size increases. At the lower end the loss is heavy in fields of 5-7 runners, which improves slightly for 8-11 runner races then returns an excellent profit for fields with at least 12 runners. Essentially these races are "matches" with only two possible winners: the favourite and second favourite. Unfortunately there are very few of these contests during the course of the season. The 64p profit in Figure 6 was generated by just nine qualifiers, although it should be noted that all nine finished in the frame.

Figure 6: **Average return for each way bets placed on the second favourite by price and field size for non-handicap races featuring an odds on favourite**

Price of 2nd Favourite	Number of Runners					
	5-7	8-11	12-15	16-20	21+	All
Ev-2/1	-£0.21	-£0.01	+£0.64			-£0.08
9/4-10/3	+£0.05	+£0.20	-£0.11	-£0.13		+£0.09
7/2-5/1	-£0.19	-£0.10	-£0.10	+£0.16	+£1.33	-£0.12
11/2-9/1	+£0.09	-£0.15	-£0.03	-£0.77	+£0.40	-£0.10
10/1-22/1	+£0.30	-£0.76	-£1.00	-£1.00		-£0.54
All Prices	-£0.07	-£0.05	-£0.04	-£0.38	+£1.02	-£0.07

According to Figure 6, in small fields featuring an odds on favourite it is possible to return a 9p/£1 profit by backing all second favourites priced between 11/2 and 9/1 each way. This profit was based on 68 qualifiers making it a worthwhile option to consider. For second favourites priced between 10/1 and 22/1 another good profit was returned, but with only five qualifiers this can be discounted, similarly the profit from large fields (i.e. 21 runners or more) is due to a small sample.

The most reliable profit in the table may be found in the group identified by second favourites priced between 9/4 and 10/3. A profit of 9p for every £1 staked would have been sufficient to cover the old off-course tax, and it is based on a total of 252 qualifiers of which almost 70% generated a return by finishing in the frame. The bulk of this profit came from the 85 qualifiers in the 8-11 runner category for which the equivalent win return was just 11p per £1. Clearly this type of bet could form the basis for either a system in its own right or as a "saver" bet.

When the favourite in a non-handicap is priced in the evens to 2/1 range a very different picture emerges. The first important characteristic of these races is that simply backing the favourite returns a profit when the field size exceeds 20. For win singles this profit has averaged 21p for every £1 staked over the past four seasons (32 bets), with the equivalent return for each way betting just 12p. Following the second favourite in these big field races would also have been profitable. However, unlike the findings in the previous section, the each way return is significantly less than the win return for these horses, just 2p per £1 compared to 18p for the win bet.

Extending the analysis to cover races where the favourite started in the 9/4 to 10/3 range produces similar results. The favourite is worth following in races with 16 or more runners returning a profit from the sample of 196 races of 18p for every £1 when backed to win and 4p for every £1 placed each way. Figure 7 shows the average return for the second favourite backed to win and each way.

Figure 7: Average return for win and each way bets placed on the second favourite by price and field size for non-handicap races featuring a favourite priced between 9/4 and 10/3

Price of 2nd Favourite		Number of Runners					
		5-7	8-11	12-15	16-20	21+	All
9/4-10/3	Average Win Return	+£0.07	-£0.05	-£0.19	+£0.05	-£1.00	-£0.05
	Average EW Return	-£0.02	-£0.07	-£0.14	+£0.11	-£0.73	-£0.07
7/2-5/1	Average Win Return	-£0.60	-£0.07	+£0.13	+£0.22	-£0.11	+£0.00
	Average EW Return	-£0.37	-£0.07	-£0.02	+£0.09	-£0.06	-£0.05
11/2-9/1	Average Win Return	-£1.00	+£0.62	+£0.29	+£0.23	+£1.05	+£0.40
	Average EW Return	-£1.00	+£0.39	+£0.18	-£0.07	+£0.65	+£0.18
All Price (Win Bets)		-£0.10	-£0.05	+£0.05	+£0.19	+£0.20	+£0.01
All Prices (EW Bets)		-£0.11	-£0.06	-£0.03	+£0.06	+£0.12	-£0.04

Again fields with 16 or more runners provide a profitable betting medium for the second favourite, with a return of 19p per £1 for the win bet and 7p per £1 for the each way bet. Interestingly this is markedly different from the results of races with an odds on favourite which suggest the each way bet is more profitable. However, with respect to the consistency of the two betting approaches, of the 196 selections in races with 16 or more runners the second favourite won 43 times but made the frame on 102 occasions.

Another informative feature of Figure 7 is the good profit figures for horses priced between 11/2 and 9/1. Simply backing the second favourite under these conditions produced a profit of 40p for every £1 staked, the equivalent each way profit was 18p for the 89 races.

Clearly there are occasions where win betting is more profitable, but in many cases the each way approach may well be the better option.

Each Way Doubles

Each way doubles are popular bets for several reasons. An each way double not only appears to be a "safe" bet, but it also promises the chance to win a substantial amount for a modest stake. For example, two 9-4 selections coupled in an each way double only need to make the frame for the bettor to make a profit, and if they both win the return is equivalent to an 11/2 winner.

On this basis making a profit from each way doubles seems to be certain. However, it is not quite so straightforward. A random sample of horses priced at 9-4 and combined in each way doubles returns a loss of approximately 20p for every £1 staked. So although the bet looks easy to win, in practice this is not the case.

In the past the main advantage to the each way double concerned the off-course tax. For this bet the tax was only paid on the initial stake, whereas backing a horse singularly then reinvesting the return on a second horse would have required the bettor to pay tax on both bets, increasing the likelihood of long term failure. Nowadays off-course betting tax is no longer an issue so the bet can be placed as singles which mean the bettor does not need to find two horses running on a single day. Providing accurate records are kept the each way double may take place over several racing days.

In the previous section a potentially profitable system was identified that required backing the second favourite when priced between 9/4 and 10/3 each way in non-handicaps featuring an odds on favourite (Figure 6). This may also be a suitable system for bettors favouring the each way double. Naturally there will not be many races that meet this criterion each day, so in the past this would not have been a viable betting option, but due to the abolition of off-course tax it is now possible.

So does combining pairs of selections identified by the previous system into each way doubles improve the overall return? To test this bet it is necessary to randomly order the selections and then combine them into pairs. This simulation can then be repeated several times with each repetition producing one average return figure relating to the return from betting all of the combinations in each way doubles. This figure can then be compared to the each way single return of 9p per £1 staked.

The standard approach to an each way double is to consider the bet in two parts, win and place, with the win return from the first horse becoming the stake to win on the second and similarly the place return from the first horse becomes the place stake for the second. This is generally referred to as "win to win, place to place" betting. However, in practice this would only be achievable if the two horses ran on the same day, or via a bookmaker that accepts place only betting because if the first horse made the frame but did not win there would only be a place stake to carry forward to the other selection. As an alternative, bookmakers also accept "equally divided" each way doubles. For this bet the total return from the first horse is divided equally to form the two parts of the bet on the second horse. So a £10.00 return from the first selection would be placed £5.00 each way on the next. Naturally this type of bet can be placed without regard to the time between races. The results of this simulation are given in Figure 8.

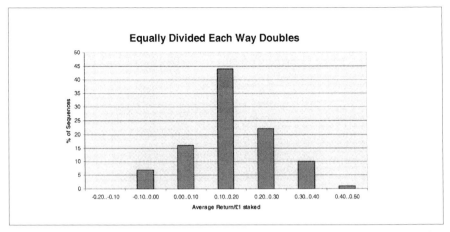

Figure 8: Distribution of the average return for the 100 simulations of the each way double option.

From the 100 simulations the overall average return was 17p per £1 staked and the median figure was also 17p, significantly higher than the 9p returned from betting each way singles. From the graph it can be seen that the bulk of the simulations resulted in a profit of between 10p and 20p, with the best return exceeding 40p. However, it should also be noted that using each way doubles can reduce a profitable approach to a losing one. For seven of the simulations the final return was negative, thus emphasising the effect of the order of the results on the outcome of the strategy.

For comparative purposes the results of the same 100 simulations are given in Figure 9 for each way doubles placed in the traditional format of win to win, place to place.

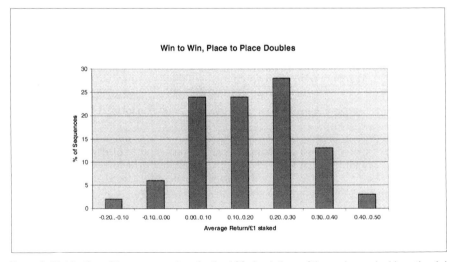

Figure 9: Distribution of the average return for the 100 simulations of the each way double option (win to win, place to place betting).

From Figure 9 it can be seen that the distribution is more widely spread than in the previous example implying a wider range of outcomes. At the lower end two simulations produce an average return of less than -10p per £1 staked, and a further six also produce a negative result. However, the overall average was similar to the previous equally divided example at just over 17p, with a slightly higher median figure. Whether the bettor chooses this option over the previous one is dependent on his/her attitude towards risk. Essentially the equally divided bet is more likely to produce a long term profit and can be considered the more conservative approach.

Another important aspect of the each way double is that the total risk is lower since the total stake is lower. For this example, using a 1 point stake, backing all 252 selections as each way singles would result in a total outlay of 252 points, whereas combining them into pairs for each way doubles would risk a total of 126 points. This needs to be considered when comparing betting strategies to initial bank sizes.

Conclusion

The aim of this article is to investigate the differences between win and each way betting. Using a sample of races taken from four seasons various tables and graphs seem to indicate that, in contrast to the theoretical model, each way betting is the more profitable option. Naturally an examination such as this only considers the general view, whether an individual win bettor should modify his/her strategy to include each way betting depends very much on the style of betting. The only way to be sure such a move would be productive is to analyse previous bets and compare the outcome. However, the findings detailed in this article do suggest that such a comparison could well be worthwhile.

CHAPTER 5
SYSTEMS – DEVELOPMENT AND IMPLEMENTATION

Everyone interested in horserace betting either uses a system or knows someone who does. This may seem to be an over-generalisation but it is nonetheless true. Systems are a very popular betting method. As opposed to form study, they are easy to use and take very little time to check each day, which is a major advantage for those who do not rely 100% on the sport for income.

The bulk of the work is undertaken during a period of system development resulting in one or several systems which can then be employed during the season. Another advantage with this approach is that systems can be precisely structured. This rigid style allows them to be tested against known race results and thus provides the bettor with invaluable information regarding their likely performance. Unfortunately this level of rigidity can be a drawback since it does not allow the system to develop and adapt to changing circumstances.

Like many things in life, systems are based on past experience. The developer either uses his/her personal knowledge of the sport to generate a system, or uses a more structured technique based on an analysis of previous results. This latter approach is often referred to as back-fitting since it requires the fitting of a system (or rule) to historical results. The method is very effective, but like any form of retrospective analysis, it needs to be conducted and validated in an unbiased manner to achieve the best results.

Horseracing Systems

A requirement of a horseracing system is that it should be able to be written as a rule that is unambiguous and straightforward to apply. The system should also generate an acceptable success rate and return a profit. But, most importantly, the system should be likely to reproduce its good historical performance in future races.

To satisfy the first objective the system should rely on quantifiable variables, such as the number of days since the horse last raced or its position in the betting market. Qualitative variables, such as suitability of the going, or race distance, should be avoided unless they can be defined precisely. These opinion-based variables are always difficult to validate and often their assessment does not remain constant over time.

Simple systems are always preferred to highly complex ones. A simple system consisting of just a few conditions is easy to implement and hence more likely to be applied correctly. Furthermore, these systems tend to be more general requiring less data to validate them and are less prone to over-fitting. Though highly refined systems map the historical data more precisely, they may not perform as well in the future.

Ideally the system will also be unique. Using the usual data items in a conventional fashion is unlikely to return a long term profit. However, a new relationship between the data and the odds is more likely to return a profit since it will not already have been accounted for in the prices on offer.

Finally, the system must be structured so that the bettor is able to implement it. It is no good developing a highly profitable system that cannot be implemented. For instance someone who is employed full time may not be able to monitor the betting shows closely and so would not be able to run a system with such a requirement. This may appear to be obvious, but it is surprising the number of systems that are developed without thought for how they are going to be run.

Developing Horseracing Systems

Although it is possible to identify specific combinations of variables which return a long term profit as a result of general form study, the most common approach to systems development is data mining.

Data mining methods require a data set containing historical results which include all of the critical factors. This is a key step in the whole process. It is necessary for the systems developer to base his/her work on a data set that is representative of the domain, accurate and unbiased. This may seem obvious. However, it is not necessarily a straightforward task to undertake, especially when extracting the data manually from a formbook. Furthermore it is important to use data from more than a single season. Seasonal variations need to be accounted for in any system, thus a data set covering three or more seasons is desirable.

The data mining process then requires the analyst to search the data for profitable relationships between the data elements. Consequently, the search is driven by the profit variable. With form study the result is generally the horse with the highest chance of success, the bettor can then convert these findings into acceptable prices before considering a bet. However, with system development the target is profit from the outset and this changes the way the variables need to be viewed. When analysing a race with the aim of determining the most likely winner, the factors considered generally have a linear relationship with the outcome of the race. For instance, the higher the speed rating, with respect to the other runners, the greater the chance of success; the higher the trainer's success rate the more likely the horse is to win and so on. With systems development the relationships that need to be considered change from linear to non-linear simply because the target variable is not chance of success but profit.

The betting market mirrors the horse's chance of winning and the more likely a horse is to win the shorter the price on offer will be. Consequently a horse with ideal credentials is unlikely to be on offer at a value price. This also applies to horses at the other end of the market where again the odds will understate the chance of success. The aim of a system is to find a combination of factors which generate a profit in the long term. This may require the bettor to invest in horses which are far from the most likely winning candidates.

Although the combination of variables that constitute a system may not match the idealistic view of horserace analysis, they must still be logical. However, this logic is not based on conventional approaches, but with respect to the profit/loss statistics. So, in other words, a profitable system may have as a condition that the horse has been unraced for over 100 days. This defies the conventional logic which dictates that horses returning from a long course absence are less likely to be fit and hence less likely to win. However, the system view is that these horses are more likely to be over-priced by the market simply due to this factor and the general assessment of its importance by the betting public. So although it may at first seem illogical to include such a condition, it is in fact a sensible factor to include when considered in the context of the profit/loss variable.

Developing a System – An Example Using Sensitivity Analysis

The easiest way to develop a horseracing system is to identify an initial key variable (or base factor), and then build the system around it. This initial factor may be something as simple as a rating, or it may be more complex such as good horses running below par. Once identified the race results should be analysed with respect to this key variable to determine a benchmark profit/loss value, and then the other factors considered in turn to determine whether they make any significant improvement to this benchmark figure. However, with detailed databases examining the other variables is a time consuming task, and the simplest method is to adopt sensitivity analysis approach.

Sensitivity analysis is used in many different numerical disciplines, and essentially it monitors how a system reacts to changes in its influencing variables. For horseracing systems, the initial condition is fixed and the other critical variables allowed to vary across their entire range with profit and loss figures calculated for each value. Naturally the easiest way to present this analysis is in graphical form.

As an example consider the following system which takes the top-rated horses, based on speed figures, in novice and maiden hurdle races as the base factor. Over the four seasons 1998/99-2001/02, these horses returned a level stake profit at starting price of 7p for every £1 staked on the 2014 races. This is an excellent starting point, and in fact could be used as the system itself since a 7% return is not insignificant and a success rate of 31% is more than acceptable. However, it is always desirable to check other influences in case the system can be improved without losing any generality.

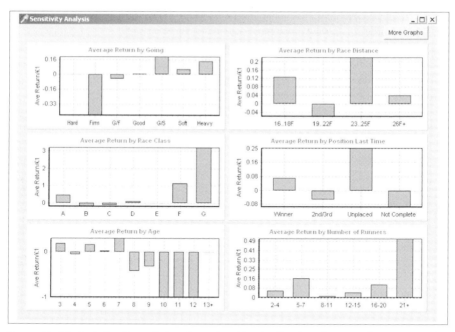

Screen Shot 1: Analysis of top rated novice and maiden hurdlers by going, race distance, race class, position last time, age and field size

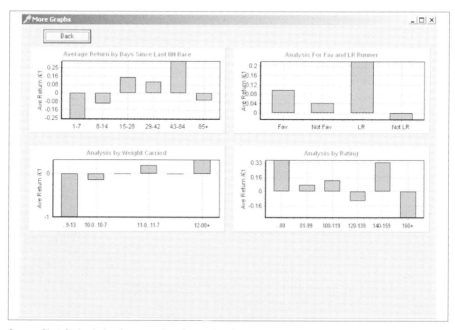

Screen Shot 2: Analysis of top rated novice and maiden hurdlers by days since last jumps race, market position, weight carried and speed rating

Sensitivity analysis produces the graphs presented in the screen shots. The graphs show the performance of the top-rated horses with respect to each of the other critical variables. Interestingly, the effect of the non-linearity is immediately visible. Conventional form study states that winning recent form is preferred. However, from the graph it is apparent that horses which finished unplaced on their latest start are favoured over winners, simply based on the level of profit. Applying this one condition reduces the number of races to 625 but increases the profit to 25p for every £1 staked. The overall success rate does drop to just over 20% though, which may be too low for some bettors so this condition is reset and ignored at this stage of the process.

A more interesting influence is weight carried. The profit increases as the weight increases and setting a lower limit of 11-00 produces a profit of 16p per £1 staked for 1124 races with a success rate of 38%. Leaving this condition as part of the system and reapplying the sensitivity analysis produces graphs which show that although horses unplaced on their latest start return the best profit, all previous race positions now return a good profit. However, the profit is low for horses making a quick return, and negative for those off the track for over 84 days, which is again evidence of the non-linearity involved which this type of analysis. More importantly the profit is negative for all horses aged 8 or more (see Screen Shot 3). Restricting the system to just horses aged between three-years-old and seven-years-old produces 412 winners from 1047 bets and a profit of 21p for every £1 staked.

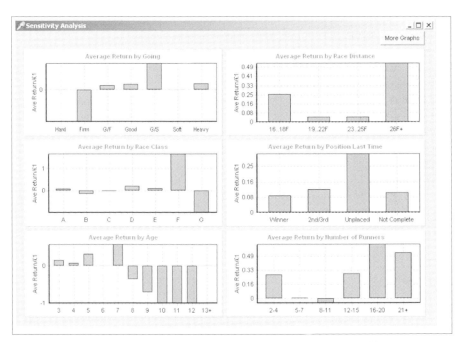

Screen Shot 3: Analysis of top rated novice and maiden hurdlers set to carry 11-00 or more by going, race distance, race class, position last time, age and field size

This is now a reasonably general system with an acceptable success rate (39%) and an excellent profit margin. The conditions are sensible and not overly specific, though the addition of a maximum days off the course condition would improve the return the level of improvement would be only minimal. Consequently this system would appear to be worth following and could be validated against a new data set, and analysed by season as final checks before implementation.

Underlying Influences – Hidden Factors

In 1936 the Literary Digest published the results of a poll designed to forecast the result of the forthcoming American presidential election. The poll indicated that Alfred Langdon would win the election with 370 votes; his opponent, Franklin D. Roosevelt, was expected to receive only 61 votes. In fact the election results produced 523 votes for Roosevelt; Langdon secured a paltry eight. Clearly the poll was misleading.

The error here was far from intentional and lay in the incorrect method of sampling employed. As opposed to sampling the views of the public in a conventional way, the pollsters decided to conduct a telephone poll. In 1930s America the telephone was a rare commodity and only the very rich normally had access to one at home. These tended to support Langdon which resulted in a bias in the poll results.

There are very often connections, in statistical terms, between sets of information which are not fully realised. In the previous example, the company conducting the poll had not appreciated that people that owned telephones were not representative of the country and that they were likely to provide a biased sample.

The same can happen in horseracing systems with third party variables affecting the outcome of the system for reasons the system developer does not fully understand. This can lead to invalid systems which suddenly under-perform for no apparent reason. A change in race structuring may not appear to have any bearing on a system, yet this apparently unrelated variable could be affecting the results. Furthermore, an understanding of the relationships can produce more meaningful analyses of the races and produce more reliable systems.

As an example, consider the novice hurdle system developed in an earlier section:

> all novices' and maiden hurdle races
> top rated on speed figures
> age of horse less than 8
> weight carried 11-00 or more

This simple four condition system generally produces around 250 selections per year, and returns a profit of about 20p for every £1 staked at starting price.

The four conditions of the system seem relatively straightforward, using variables that are very common in system development. Speed figures can be very useful when applied to National Hunt racing, providing they are based on accurate time and distance information. In this instance speed figures are used to identify the horse with most proven ability in the race. The age condition eliminates older horses that tend to under-perform in these race grades. Though a few older horses can run well in these races, in general an eight-year-old with ability should no longer be qualified for a novices' event having won hurdle races previously. Those which are tend to be either poor or unreliable animals.

The eight-year-old Ad Hoc is the obvious exception. After a period running over fences, winning such races as the Whitbread Handicap Chase at Sandown, he returned to hurdle racing in the 2002-2003 season and showed he still possessed the speed and ability to win over the smaller obstacles. However, horses such as Ad Hoc are very much the exception, in fact horses aged eight or more win less than 4% of all novices' hurdle races at a success rate of about one in twenty.

Whilst the age requirement is easy to justify, the weight condition affects the system in more subtle ways. In handicap races horses carrying more weight tend to win more often and this variable can be an important discriminating factor in systems. However, novices' and maiden hurdle races are not handicaps, and horses are not assigned different weights based on their ability. The weight each horse carries is dependent on such factors as the race conditions, the age of the horse, jockey's allowance, gender and, in the case of novices' events, previous wins. Though maiden hurdle races feature only horses that have not previously won a hurdle race, novices' events can include runners that have won several similar events. These horses are awarded penalties depending on the value of the races they have won (as opposed to ability) and can increase their weight they need to carry by up to 14 lbs.

The weight condition would not exclude previous winners since, in most cases, the penalties they are set to carry would increase their weight above the 11-00 limit. However, it does bias the selection against younger horses when they compete in all-aged races. Also mares would be less likely to be selected when racing against geldings and in many cases it would rule out horses ridden by conditional jockeys. So although the condition relates directly to weight, its effect is due, in the main, to other conditions. Consequently the system could be revised with each of these factors analysed in detail. For instance, the races could be partitioned into those where mares race against geldings and separate analyses performed, the results of which may improve the performance of the original system.

However, this will make the system more complex to apply and could result in over-fitting. In other words, the system becomes too specific and although it produces good results historically, does not continue to perform well in the future. This is the main drawback using back-fitting to generate profitable systems. Whilst a system may work well, it is important to be aware of the effect of underlying variables and although it may not be necessary to modify the system, such variables need to be considered carefully with respect to other changing conditions that could affect the results of the method.

Validating Systems

Back-fitting is a biased approach to generating systems and, as a result, can produce inappropriate rules that do not perform well in future events. For instance the system could be very specific producing rules that refer to small areas of the data which, in the past, were profitable but are highly likely to be unprofitable in the future. Also the system may rely on a few large priced winners to generate the positive return that have been found by repeatedly refining and filtering of the data. Such systems are unlikely to continue to produce a profit and should be avoided. Given this weakness in the system development approach, it is necessary to validate any system carefully before implementation.

If back-fitting has been used, the best way to validate the system is by using a new data set. Before developing the system it is necessary to partition the data set and use one part for development and another for validation. Normally this partition is performed randomly, but given that horseracing is time dependent (i.e. races, horse training methods etc change over time) a more effective partition is achieved by simply using the most recent data for validation. With five years data, the usual approach would be to use the first four years to develop the system and the fifth year to validate any rule.

There will be cases where, due to lack of data, it is not possible to reserve a complete season for validation. Under these circumstances other approaches to validation are required. The most common method would be a statistical approach, specifically a confidence interval. If applied to a randomly selected sample, the confidence interval provides a range in which the average of the population from which the sample was selected will fall. For instance, the results of opinion polls are normally supplemented with a confidence interval such as 38% ± 4% which shows the degree of error associated with the estimate.

For this method to work well, the sample needs to be selected from the whole population, which is not possible for horseracing since this would need to include the future races in which we would like to support the system's qualifiers. Consequently this approach should not be relied upon to provide a guarantee of the system achieving a predetermined level. Its value is to determine systems that are unlikely to perform well. Any system that has a confidence interval with a lower limit close to zero should be viewed with a degree of doubt and if followed stakes should be kept to a minimum until sufficient data are accrued that support the system.

Another form of validation that should be applied in addition to the methods mentioned previously, is an analysis of the performance of the system over shorter time periods. This is easily represented graphically as a rolling average. The data on which the system was developed together with the test data from the population on which the rolling average is based.

To calculate the rolling average it is necessary to set a sample size, s, for instance. The average return for the system based on the first s qualifiers is calculated and plotted on the graph. The first qualifier is then dropped and the s+1 qualifier added to the sample. The average is again calculated and the point plotted on the graph. This continues until all of the qualifiers have been used. The resulting graph illustrates how the performance of the system has varied over time and shows the highs and lows that can be expected to be repeated.

A further advantage of this approach is that it highlights potentially important patterns in the data which are not apparent from the statistical measure of confidence. For instance the system may have worked well for a period of time then deteriorated significantly. The confidence interval may still indicate a profit, but from the graph of the system's performance it would be clear that the system was unlikely to perform well in the future.

As an example Screen Shot 4 shows the various methods of validation for the novice hurdle system discussed earlier.

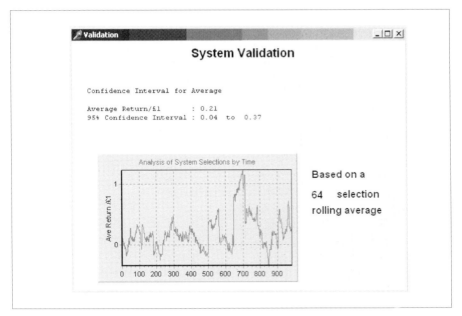

Screen Shot 4: Validation of a horseracing system

Screen Shot 4 shows the average return for the system, in this case 21p/£1 staked; the confidence interval 4p to 37p and the rolling average graph for the 1047 system qualifiers. The lower limit of the confidence interval is relatively close to zero and indicates that this system may produce a negative return in the future. The graph shows the average return for each consecutive set of 64 bets. The low point, around bet 850, was during the Foot and Mouth crisis and showed that the system did not perform well under these unusual circumstances. (Again this illustrated how systems can be susceptible to changing circumstances not previously considered.) However, the majority of 64-bet samples produce a profitable outcome, so on this alone I would consider the system to be worth following.

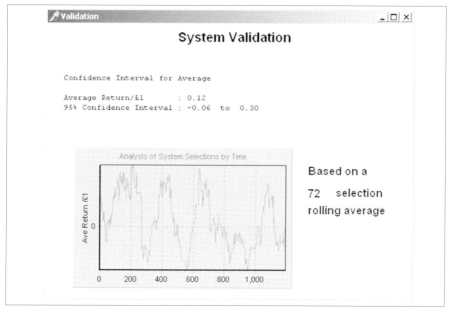

Screen Shot 5: Validation of an unreliable horseracing system

Screen shot 5 shows the validation output for a less reliable system.

Though the average return at 12p for every £1 staked is reasonable, the confidence interval ranging from -6p to 30p is not particularly encouraging. Furthermore the graph shows that for a vast number of 72-bet samples the return would be negative, consequently there would be too many occasions through the season when the system was appearing to perform poorly. Under these conditions the bettor is unlikely to continue with the rule and losses would be sustained. Given this information I would not be prepared to follow this particular system. However, the cyclical nature of the graph suggests that a time-based factor may be unduly influencing the system's performance so further analysis may be worthwhile.

Implementing Horseracing Systems

When developing the system, success rate may not appear to be important. After all the main aim is to return a good profit so providing this is achieved the rate at which the system identifies winning bets is irrelevant. However, once a system is running its success rate becomes a crucial factor.

The problem facing most system followers is whether to continue with a system that is performing poorly with long losing runs. Naturally this is more likely to happen if the system has a low success rate. For instance a system with a 10% success rate is very likely to produce a losing run of more than twenty bets during a run of 200 bets.

The worst response to a losing run is to stop playing the system. Providing the system is well-founded, and adequately tested, there is no need to doubt that it will return a profit at the end of the season providing other conditions remain stable. Systems have good and poor runs, this is only to be expected, so unless there are significant changes to the conditions that impact on the system it should be followed for the predetermined time period. During the Foot and Mouth crisis of a couple of years ago, system players were well advised to stop following their methods, simply because this unexpected outbreak had a significant impact on the structure and results of races. Under normal circumstances this action should be avoided in order to give the method a chance to recover.

In order to avoid long losing runs, it is preferable to follow systems that possess a high success rate. As a guide, a 20% success rate is considered a minimum, and one method to ensure this outcome is to restrict the system to qualifiers that are priced nearer the front of the market. As an example, a maximum price of the qualifiers can be set to a relatively low figure, such as 9/1.

Other methods include staking plans that reduce the stake for the longer priced qualifiers, but these staking methods need to be fully accounted for in the system development and validation phases.

CHAPTER 6
FAVOURITES TO FOLLOW

Whereas many value punters would accept the idea of following the draw as a valid betting approach, the majority would probably query a method based on favourites. In fact in one racing book the author states that "by definition the favourite is not a value bet". Clearly this is nonsense, though it is a view that some accept. There are poor value favourites, but by the same token there are good value favourites, as with all aspects of horseracing the problem is identifying which is which.

In general terms the favourite is often better priced that the outsiders. Table 1 shows the average return for a selection of flat races, in each case the favourite returns a greater proportion of the stake to punters. So if the favourite is indeed a poor value bet, then the non-favourites offer even poorer value.

Table 1: The Performance of Absolute Favourites by Race Grade

Race Grade	Favourite				Non Favourite			
	Wins	Runs	%	Ret/£1	Wins	Runs	%	Ret/£1
3-y.o Maiden Races	331	778	42.5%	-£0.08	486	7335	6.6%	-£0.43
All-Age Maiden Races	301	651	46.2%	-£0.04	385	6147	6.3%	-£0.54
3-y.o Claiming Races	34	123	30.1%	-£0.18	101	1450	7.0%	-£0.28
3-y.o Handicaps	329	1231	26.7%	-£0.09	1041	15972	6.5%	-£0.31

The important feature of any systematic betting approach based on favourites is the high win ratio. Draw-based techniques, for instance, result in high priced winners and long losing runs, so from a psychological perspective these methods can be very difficult to follow. After a run of 15 losing bets it is not so easy to back another 33/1 apparent no-hoper just because he has been allotted a specific stall that in that past has proved profitable to follow.

The success rate for methods based on the market leaders usually exceed 50%, so when these methods are employed alongside low win rate techniques the winning favourites help to break up the long losing runs and often change a day's betting from no winners from four bets to three winners from eight. Psychologically this is a significant improvement even if the day returns a loss overall.

Betting systems can range from the simple one item method to the highly complex system incorporating functions of several variables. And systems based on favourites are no different.

However, I have found that the simple approaches are often the best, so in the following section a number of profitable systems based on favourites are presented. For each system the average return is based on a level £1 staked at starting price, a figure of +£0.09 would have been necessary to cover the old off-course tax at 9%. Like all systems, whilst these methods have worked well in the past there is no guarantee they will continue to do so, especially in a sport changing as much as racing. However, they do highlight potentially profitable areas which are worthy of close attention.

Favourites to Follow – Turf Flat Racing

The following tables are based on the five Flat racing seasons to end 2003. Weight carried is the actual weight carried including adjustments for the jockey's claim and overweight as opposed to the weight allocated. Unplaced refers to horses finishing out of the first three in any field size. All-Age races are those which are not specifically restricted to juveniles or three-year-olds.

Juvenile Group 1 Races – Absolute Favourites

Attribute	Wins	Runs	Win Rate	Ave. Return/£1
Days Since Last Run: 29..60	7	10	70.0%	+£0.46
Starting Price: up to 2/1	13	22	59.1%	+£0.24
Position on Latest Run: First, 2nd, 3rd	11	20	55.0%	+£0.15

Juvenile Group 2 Races – Absolute Favourites

Attribute	Wins	Runs	Win Rate	Ave. Return/£1
Starting Price: Odds On	7	10	70.0%	+£0.19

Juvenile Listed Races – Absolute Favourites

Attribute	Wins	Runs	Win Rate	Ave. Return/£1
BHB rating: 90..99	6	14	42.9%	+£0.57
Days Since Last Run: 29..100	14	28	50.0%	+£0.55
Starting Price: Evens – 2/1	27	60	45.0%	+£0.20
Position on Latest Run: Unplaced	5	13	38.5%	+£0.25

Juvenile Stakes Races – Absolute Favourites

Attribute	Wins	Runs	Win Rate	Ave. Return/£1
BHB rating: 90..109	42	84	50.0%	+£0.09
Weight Carried: 9-8..10-00	4	4	100.0%	+£0.60
Days Since Last Run: 101+	4	5	90.0%	+£0.50
Position on Latest Run: Unplaced	44	95	46.3%	+£0.13

Juvenile Claiming Races – Absolute Favourites

Attribute	Wins	Runs	Win Rate	Ave. Return/£1
BHB rating: 70 .. 89	5	10	50.0%	+£0.32
Days Since Last Run: 1..14	28	53	52.8%	+£0.49
Starting Price: Odds On	11	13	84.6%	+£0.42
Starting Price: 9/4 – 4/1	12	36	33.3%	+£0.27
Position on Latest Run: 2nd or 3rd	11	26	42.3%	+£0.24
Position on Latest Run: Unplaced	19	49	38.8%	+£0.15

Juvenile Maiden Races – Absolute Favourites

Attribute	Wins	Runs	Win Rate	Ave. Return/£1
BHB rating: 50..109	97	201	48.3%	+£0.14

Juvenile Selling Races – Absolute Favourites

Attribute	Wins	Runs	Win Rate	Ave. Return/£1
Weight Carried: 8-08..9-07	39	114	34.2%	+£0.10
Days Since Last Run: 8..14	32	88	36.4%	+£0.10
Starting Price: 9/4 – 4/1	32	100	32.0%	+£0.26
Position on Latest Run: Unplaced	42	116	36.2%	+£0.14

Juvenile Handicaps – Absolute Favourites

Attribute	Wins	Runs	Win Rate	Ave. Return/£1
Starting Price: Ev – 2/1	61	148	41.2%	+£0.08

3-Y.O Group 1 Races – Absolute Favourites

Attribute	Wins	Runs	Win Rate	Ave. Return/£1
Weight Carried: 9-0..9-07	11	31	35.5%	+£0.16
Days Since Last Run: 15..60	9	21	42.9%	+£0.38
Position on Latest Run: First, 2nd, 3rd	10	25	40.0%	+£0.32

3-Y.O Group 2 Races – Absolute Favourites

Attribute	Wins	Runs	Win Rate	Ave. Return/£1
All Absolute Favourites	6	18	33.0%	+£0.12

3-Y.O Stakes Races – Absolute Favourites

Attribute	Wins	Runs	Win Rate	Ave. Return/£1
Days Since Last Run: 101+	30	62	48.4%	+£0.07

3-Y.O Claiming Races – Absolute Favourites

Attribute	Wins	Runs	Win Rate	Ave. Return/£1
Days Since Last Run: 29..60	12	25	48.0%	+£0.34
Starting Price: Odds On	12	18	66.7%	+£0.16

3-Y.O Maiden Races – Absolute Favourites

Attribute	Wins	Runs	Win Rate	Ave. Return/£1
Days Since Last Run: 1..7	9	17	52.9%	+£0.16

3-Y.O Selling Races – Absolute Favourites

Attribute	Wins	Runs	Win Rate	Ave. Return/£1
BHB rating: 50 .. 69	25	61	41.0%	+£0.28
Price: Ev - 2/1	12	27	44.4%	+£0.09

3-Y.O Handicaps – Absolute Favourites

Attribute	Wins	Runs	Win Rate	Ave. Return/£1
Weight Carried: 9-8..10-00	22	44	50.0%	+£0.10

All-Age Group 1 Races – Absolute Favourites

Attribute	Wins	Runs	Win Rate	Ave. Return/£1
Weight Carried: 9-8..10-00	3	3	10.0%	+£1.98
Days: 61..100	5	10	50.0%	+£0.42

All-Age Group 2 Races – Absolute Favourites

Attribute	Wins	Runs	Win Rate	Ave. Return/£1
Age: 6yo	4	7	57.1%	+£0.51

All-Age Group 3 Races – Absolute Favourites

Attribute	Wins	Runs	Win Rate	Ave. Return/£1
Age: 3yo	21	40	52.5%	+£0.23
Age: 5yo	11	25	44.0%	+£0.52
BHB rating: 120..139	4	8	50.0%	+£0.66
Starting Price: Evens – 2/1	24	57	42.1%	+£0.08
Position on Latest Run: Unplaced	10	27	37.0%	+£0.13

All-Age Listed Races – Absolute Favourites

Attribute	Wins	Runs	Win Rate	Ave. Return/£1
BHB rating: 120..139	5	6	83.3%	+£0.38

All-Age Stakes Races – Absolute Favourites

Attribute	Wins	Runs	Win Rate	Ave. Return/£1
Age: 8yo	10	25	40.0%	+£0.42
BHB rating: 110..119	43	73	58.9%	+£0.16

All-Age Claiming Races – Absolute Favourites

Attribute	Wins	Runs	Win Rate	Ave. Return/£1
BHB rating : 90..99	10	20	50.0%	+£0.25
Weight Carried: 9-08+	54	125	43.2%	+£0.13
Days Since Last Run: 1..7	35	93	37.6%	+£0.07
Position on Latest Run: Won	38	81	46.9%	+£0.19

All-Age Maiden Races – Absolute Favourites

Attribute	Wins	Runs	Win Rate	Ave. Return/£1
BHB rating: 90..99	26	38	68.4%	+£0.24

All-Age Selling Races – Absolute Favourites

Attribute	Wins	Runs	Win Rate	Ave. Return/£1
Age: 3yo	15	42	35.7%	+£0.15
Age: 6yo	10	23	43.5%	+£0.37

All-Age Listed (Rated) Handicaps – Absolute Favourites

Attribute	Wins	Runs	Win Rate	Ave. Return/£1
Age: 4yo	5	15	33.3%	+£0.27
Starting Price: 9/4 – 4/1	8	22	36.4%	+£0.50
Position on Latest Run: 2nd or 3rd	4	12	33.3%	+£0.17
Position on Latest Run: Unplaced	4	10	40.0%	+£0.56

Favourites to Follow – NH Racing

The following results, which are sub-divided by race type, are taken from five seasons of Jumps races. References to weight carried and finishing positions are the same as for the Flat tables.

Novices' Hurdle Races – Absolute Favourites

Attribute	Wins	Runs	Win Rate	Ave. Return/£1
Weight Carried: 12-01+	10	14	71.4%	+£0.15
Weight Carried: 11-8..12-00	192	315	60.9%	+£0.09
Days Since last Run: 1..7	59	110	53.6%	+£0.13
Position on Latest Run: Unplaced	175	382	45.8%	+£0.07
Success Rate from Last 10 Runs: 50%+	32	44	72.7%	+£0.32

Claiming Hurdle Races – Absolute Favourites

Attribute	Wins	Runs	Win Rate	Ave. Return/£1
Age: 3yo	10	13	76.9%	+£0.88
BHB Rating: 120..129	12	21	57.1%	+£0.07
Weight Carried: 10-0..10-07	12	21	57.1%	+£0.48
Days Since Last Run: 1..7	11	16	68.8%	+£0.64

Selling Hurdle Races – Absolute Favourites

Attribute	Wins	Runs	Win Rate	Ave. Return/£1
Age: 4-8yo	123	256	48.0%	+£0.13
BHB Rating: 80..149	103	216	47.7%	+£0.17
Days Since Last Run: 1..14	39	98	40.0%	+£0.17
Starting Price: Evens - 2/1	61	123	50.0%	+£0.23
Position on Latest Run: Won	32	54	59.3%	+£0.14
Position on Latest Run: 2nd or 3rd	53	109	48.6%	+£0.18
Position on Latest Run: Pulled Up	11	19	57.9%	+£0.37

Handicap Hurdle Races – Absolute Favourites

Attribute	Wins	Runs	Win Rate	Ave. Return/£1
Weight Carried: 12-01+	7	10	70.0%	+£0.38
Days Since Last Run: 1..7	78	193	40.4%	+£0.07
Starting Price: Odds On	107	172	62.2%	+£0.06

Novices' Handicap Hurdle Races – Absolute Favourites

Attribute	Wins	Runs	Win Rate	Ave. Return/£1
BHB rating: 120..129	5	8	62.5%	+£0.78
Weight Carried: 12-01+	7	10	70.0%	+£0.40
Days Since Last Run: 101+	15	42	35.7%	+£0.19

Selling Handicap Hurdle Races – Absolute Favourites

Attribute	Wins	Runs	Win Rate	Ave. Return/£1
Position on Latest Run: Unplaced	42	160	26.3%	+£0.08

Novices' Chases – Absolute Favourites

Attribute	Wins	Runs	Win Rate	Ave. Return/£1
Age: 5yo	137	243	56.4%	+£0.10
Weight Carried: 12-01+	11	15	73.3%	+£0.32
Position on Latest Run: 2nd or 3rd	310	610	50.8%	+£0.08

Conditions Chases – Absolute Favourites

Attribute	Wins	Runs	Win Rate	Ave. Return/£1
Starting Price: Odds On	29	43	67.4%	+£0.07

Novices' Handicap Chases – Absolute Favourites

Attribute	Wins	Runs	Win Rate	Ave. Return/£1
Days Since Last Run: 101+	22	63	34.9%	+£0.15

Hunters' Chases – Absolute Favourites

Attribute	Wins	Runs	Win Rate	Ave. Return/£1
Age: 11yo	34	68	50.0%	+£0.11
Weight Carried: 11-0..11-13	31	74	41.9%	+£0.13

National Hunt Flat Races – Absolute Favourites

Attribute	Wins	Runs	Win Rate	Ave. Return/£1
Age: 6yo	49	110	44.5%	+£0.18

CHAPTER 7
CLAIMING JOCKEYS

As a rule punters have strong views regarding jockeys and their riding capabilities. And amongst any group of bettors, there would be very strong views for and against backing horses ridden by claiming jockeys trying to make their mark on the Sport. Some prefer their selections to be ridden by inexperienced jockeys simply because this often helps to lengthen the price, others steer clear of these jockeys preferring to rely on the established riders, hoping the greater experience and perhaps additional strength will more than outweigh the loss in terms of price available. Whilst both approaches are valid, there may be cases where one set of jockeys has a distinct advantage over the other.

Juvenile Turf Races

Jockey	Non-Handicap Races				Handicap Races				All Races			
	Wins	Runs	%	Ret/£1	Wins	Runs	%	Ret/£1	Wins	Runs	%	Ret/£1
Claiming Jockeys	67	879	7.6	-£0.34	28	322	8.7	-£0.13	95	1201	7.9	-£0.29
Non-Claiming Jockeys	659	6410	10.3	-£0.37	81	947	8.6	-£0.32	740	7357	10.1	-£0.37
All Jockeys	726	7289	10.0	-£0.37	109	1269	8.6	-£0.27	835	8558	9.8	-£0.36

Non - Juvenile Turf Races

Jockey	Non-Handicap Races				Handicap Races				All Races			
	Wins	Runs	%	Ret/£1	Wins	Runs	%	Ret/£1	Wins	Runs	%	Ret/£1
Claiming Jockeys	96	1446	6.6	-£0.42	375	5387	7.0	-£0.24	471	6833	6.9	-£0.28
Non-Claiming Jockeys	893	7979	11.2	-£0.34	1137	14792	7.7	-£0.32	2030	22771	8.9	-£0.32
All Jockeys	989	9425	10.5	-£0.35	1512	20179	7.5	-£0.30	2501	29604	8.4	-£0.31

Figure 1: Jockey analysis for turf flat races run in Britain showing wins-runs, success rate (%) and average return per £1 staked at starting price

From Figure 1 it can be seen that, in all races, claiming jockeys have a slightly lower success rate than their professional counterparts which would seem to imply that the weight conces-sion they receive is insufficient. However, there exist other key factors which contribute to this difference. In many cases claiming jockeys will not get to ride the better horses and therefore the likelihood of success decreases. This is apparent from the success rates given for non-handicap races: the professionals tend to score at a rate exceeding 10% whereas claiming jockeys record a success rate about 3% lower.

However, in handicaps the profile is very different. These races are designed to give all horses an equal chance of success by varying the amount of weight each runner is set to carry. Consequently this effectively normalises the differences in ability and allows a better comparison between the two sets of jockeys. Figure 1 presents the success rates for both juvenile and non-juvenile handicap races, and it can be seen that claiming jockeys record a higher win rate in the juvenile events, 8.7% compared to 8.6%. For the non-juvenile handicaps the success rates are quite close with professional jockeys winning at approximately 7.7% compared to a figure of 7.0% for apprentices and amateurs. This would seem to indicate that the level of weight allowance allocated to inexperienced jockeys is correct.

The most interesting figure for punters, though, is the average return. This value indicates the amount of money that would have been lost as a proportion of a £1 stake by backing all qualifiers at starting price. The loss incurred by following the claiming jockeys is less for both juvenile and non-juvenile handicaps. Based on these figures it could be concluded that the betting public under-estimate the ability of the riders and as a result the horses start at a better value price than for the professionally ridden animals.

Figure 2 shows comparable data for All Weather racing, and presents a very similar picture.

Juvenile AW Races

Jockey	Non-Handicap Races				Handicap Races				All Races			
	Wins	Runs	%	Ret/£1	Wins	Runs	%	Ret/£1	Wins	Runs	%	Ret/£1
Claiming Jockeys	19	216	8.8	-£0.30	9	90	10.0	-£0.42	28	306	9.2	-£0.33
Non-Claiming Jockeys	84	810	10.4	-£0.38	15	166	9.0	-£0.38	99	976	10.1	-£0.38
All Jockeys	103	1026	10.0	-£0.36	24	256	9.4	-£0.39	127	1282	9.9	-£0.37

Non-Juvenile AW Races

Jockey	Non-Handicap Races				Handicap Races				All Races			
	Wins	Runs	%	Ret/£1	Wins	Runs	%	Ret/£1	Wins	Runs	%	Ret/£1
Claiming Jockeys	89	1138	7.8	-£0.48	200	2273	8.8	-£0.28	289	3411	8.5	-£0.35
Non-Claiming Jockeys	262	2357	11.1	-£0.30	341	3713	9.2	-£0.32	603	6070	9.9	-£0.31
All Jockeys	351	3495	10.0	-£0.36	541	5986	9.0	-£0.30	892	9481	9.4	-£0.32

Figure 2: Jockey analysis for All Weather races run in Britain showing wins-runs, success rate (%) and average return per £1 staked at starting price

Given that horses ridden by apprentice and amateur jockeys offer a better rate of return than horses partnered by non-claiming jockeys, this area is worthy of further research. Figure 3 shows the number of wins, runs, and average return for all turf handicaps sub-divided by the rider's claim.

All Turf Handicaps	Jockey's Claim			
	0lbs	3lbs	5lbs	7lbs
Wins	1218	127	186	88
Runs	15739	1676	2415	1570
Success Rate (%)	7.7%	7.6%	7.7%	5.6%
Average Return/£1	-£0.32	-£0.15	-£0.21	-£0.35

Figure 3: Analysis of turf handicap races run in Britain sub-divided by the jockey's claim

Based on the data presented in Figure 3, non-claiming jockeys have recorded a success rate of 7.7%. The figures for 3lbs and 5lbs claiming jockeys are very similar. The strike rate, however, for those jockeys able to claim 7lbs drops to 5.6%. This is to be expected since this category includes jockeys with a wider variation in experience. Some will be having their first ride, whilst others will be far more experienced. For the claim to be reduced to 5lbs or lower the jockey must have had at least a set number of rides or winners. Having a fixed weight allowance at 7lbs is generally fair, but in many cases the jockeys could do with a greater weight advantage to compensate for their lack or racing experience. Consequently the success rate for these jockeys as a group is lower than for the other riders.

Again the data imply that the 3lbs and 5lbs allowances are fair, yet the prices for these runners are favourable to the punter compared to other runners. Horses ridden by non-claiming jockeys returned a loss of 32p/£1, whereas horses ridden by jockeys claiming 3lbs returned a loss of just 15p/£1. This would seem to be a reasonable starting point to develop profitable betting methods, and is certainly a feature that could be included in any handicap-based system.

Many trainers use claiming jockeys to reduce the weight burden on horses which have been allocated very high weights. Whilst this would appear to be a sound policy, the results do not support the idea.

All Horses Weighted 9-06-10-00 in Turf Handicaps	Jockey's Claim			
	0lbs	3lbs	5lbs	7lbs
Wins	365	14	18	7
Runs	3563	150	237	131
Success Rate (%)	10.2%	9.3%	7.6%	5.3%
Average Return/£1	-£0.22	-£0.24	-£0.28	-£0.56

Figure 4: Analysis of horses carrying 9-06-10-00 in turf handicap races run in Britain sub-divided by the jockey's claim

Figure 4 illustrates the success rates for horses carrying between 9st 6lbs and 10st in turf handicaps. This sample of races produces a very different profile from that given in previous examples. Non-claiming jockeys have a clear advantage, scoring at a greater frequency and returning a lower loss per bet, with these figures declining as the weight allowance increases.

Based on these findings, using claiming jockeys to reduce the weight carried by the top-weights does not improve their chances of success, in fact it reduces the likelihood of winning.

At the other end of the handicap a very different picture emerges. Figure 5 presents a summary based on a sample of turf handicap runners set to carry 8-05 or less.

All Horses Weighted	Jockey's Claim		
8-05 or less in Turf Handicaps	0lbs	3lbs	5lbs
Wins	182	57	88
Runs	3245	755	1170
Success Rate (%)	5.6%	7.5%	7.5%
Average Return/£1	-£0.37	+£0.04	-£0.09

Figure 5: Analysis of horses carrying 8-05 or less in turf handicap races run in Britain sub-divided by the jockey's claim

For the lower-weighted horses the claiming jockeys win at a higher rate than there non-claiming opponents, and for this sample at least those allocated a 3lbs allowance return a slight profit at starting price.

The Trainer Factor

Some trainers are keener to use claiming jockeys than others. This is probably influenced by the type of horse they train, the quality of the claiming jockey and the owners for which they train. A few trainers are able to exploit the weight allowance claiming jockeys receive very expertly, with a higher win ratio the result. Figure 6 presents a list of the best trainers to follow when claiming jockeys are chosen to ride in turf handicaps.

In the main the number of cases for each trainer listed in Figure 6 is relatively small, so the data are liable to fluctuate significantly. However it is interesting to note that for each trainer the success rate exceeds the average rate for non-claiming jockeys (7.7%) and for several of those listed this strike rate is more than double this figure.

Michael Bell and Mark Johnston lead the table in terms of number of runners, with 137 and 135 respectively. Their success rates are also very impressive and following both through the three seasons would have produced a good level stake profit.

However in these two cases the trainers relied very heavily on a few jockeys. For example, 81 of the 137 runners for Michael Bell were ridden by Jamie Mackay, with Keith Dalgleish riding all but 11 of Johnston's 135 runners. This is a familiar pattern. When a trainer realises that he/she has an excellent apprentice in their employment the jockey will be given plenty of rides.

Trainer	Wins	Runs	Success Rate (%)	Average Return/£1
A G Newcombe	4	36	11.1%	+£0.58
Andrew Turnell	4	25	16.0%	+£0.44
B Palling	6	47	12.8%	+£0.09
D Eddy	4	25	16.0%	+£2.32
E A Wheeler	13	82	15.9%	+£0.58
G G Margarson	4	36	11.1%	+£0.31
G M Moore	6	54	11.1%	+£0.33
I A Wood	9	68	13.2%	+£0.98
J A Glover	5	38	13.2%	+£0.63
J L Spearing	7	67	10.4%	+£0.40
J M P Eustace	4	24	16.7%	+£1.21
M C Chapman	10	90	11.1%	+£0.60

Trainer	Wins	Runs	Success Rate (%)	Average Return/£1
M Johnston	21	135	15.6%	+£0.28
M L W Bell	19	137	13.9%	+£0.21
Mrs A L M King	6	44	13.6%	+£0.15
N A Callaghan	12	72	16.7%	+£0.17
P W Hiatt	6	39	15.4%	+£0.29
R J Price	4	44	9.1%	+£0.16
S Kirk	9	71	12.7%	+£0.29
S P C Woods	4	29	13.8%	+£0.22
T D Barron	8	55	14.5%	+£0.80
T G Mills	5	20	25.0%	+£0.54

Figure 6: Analysis of 3lbs and 5lbs claiming jockeys in turf handicaps for the three seasons 2000-2002

Summary

Essentially claiming jockeys can be viewed as a positive factor when riding in handicap races, especially if their claim has been reduced to less than 7lbs. In non-handicap races, however, the picture is very different with horses ridden by claiming jockeys returning a higher loss on average than those partnered by professionals. An additional factor that needs considering is the trainer. Some have extremely profitable records with apprentice-ridden horses and these should be noted carefully.

COMPUTER MODELLING
CHAPTER 1: MODIFYING THE TRADITIONAL
FORECASTING APPROACH

Computers are now commonplace in homes, and their increased popularity has resulted in a proliferation of computer-based forecasting systems for horseracing. There will not be many horseracing enthusiasts who have not dreamt of creating a computer system that solves "the problem" and of course turns their losses into huge profits. There have even been books written on the subject, both factual and fictional. But how could such a system be developed? In this article the traditional method for system development is explored together with other approaches that improve the applicability and accuracy of the resultant systems.

Developing a Computer-Based Forecasting System for Horseracing

The initial phase of system development is to assess the problem and determine which factors should be considered when forming the solution. For the horseracing problem this simply requires the system builder to identify the variables, or inputs, the system needs to process. These vary from system to system and could include such information as ability ratings, recent form, trainer form, and the likes and dislikes of the horse with respect to the race conditions. Once identified it is necessary to find a method of representing these features in a model that the computer can easily process. Usually the model will be based on a horse-by-horse approach which takes each horse in turn and applies a weight (or scaling value) to each factor associated with the animal. The sum of these values becomes the output of the model for each horse and can be transformed into a rating or probability of success. The model outputs for each horse in a race can then be compared in order to deduce the selection. For instance a simple model may take the following form:

$$Model\ Output = x * Ability\ Rating + y * Going\ Suitability + z * Recent\ Form$$

where x, y and z are numerical weights representing the importance of each of the variables. Naturally for this structure it is necessary for the Ability Rating, Going Suitability variable, and Recent Form indicator to be represented in a numerical format. Each horse in a race is evaluated using the model and the animal with the highest model output becomes the selection.

Once the structure of the model has been defined it is necessary to generate the numerical weights that are applied to each variable. Clearly this is a critical phase of the development process, with the effectiveness of the model depending entirely on the weights chosen. So how can the weights be determined most accurately?

A common approach is to use a multiple linear regression model. The aim of this method is to find a relationship between the inputs (ability, going suitability etc) and the output (finishing position of the horse, achievement ratings etc) for a set of historical race results. This relationship indicates the level of importance of each input which can be used as weights. However, this method is only reliable if the input variables are independent. And in racing this is not usually the case: the best jockeys ride the best horses etc, consequently the variables are often related and cannot be considered to be independent.

A preferred approach is to use a neural network. These systems are easily generated and do not require the inputs to be independent. Furthermore they are often able to identify relationships between the data which had not previously been realised. Clearly this is a valuable attribute for a domain such as horseracing which has been researched exhaustively for profitable systems based on combinations of variables in recent years.

Consider the following example taken from non-juvenile flat handicaps. A neural network was trained to identify a relationship between seven inputs and one output. The inputs are: recent form (last three races), days since last run, age of horse, number of runners in the race and weight carried. The output is simply set to one for a winner and zero for a loser. The only pre-processing of the data was to limit the days since last run variable to a maximum of 200, and for the recent form to use finishing positions up to tenth. An example of this representation is given next:

Raw Data
Horse A: running fifth in a race with 23 runners
Form figures: 42561235-90021
Age: 4
Days since last run: 265
Weight allocated: 9-00

Pattern Representation

Horse Id.	Form-3	Form-2	Form-1	Days	Age	Runners	Weight	Position
A	10	2	1	200	4	23	126	0

In this example Horse A finished out of the first ten three runs ago which is represented by a 10 in the Form-3 box. The course absence of 265 days has been capped to 200, the weight carried converted to pounds, and the race result set to zero because the horse failed to win. Over 5,000 similar cases were used to train a network of the form given in Figure 1 and then tested on a new set of 4,000 similar cases, the results of which are given in Figure 2.

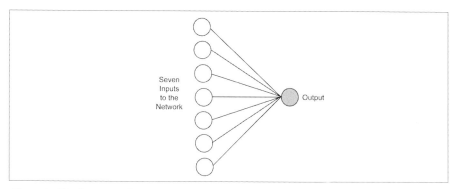

Figure 1 : The Structure of the 7-Input Neural Network

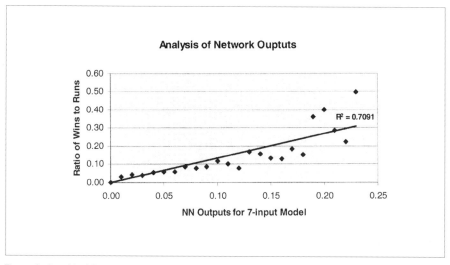

Figure 2: Graphical Representation of the Performance of the 7-Input Neural Network

From the graph (Figure 2) it can be seen that the output of the network is closely related to the chance of success. This is indicated by the trend line and the closeness of the correlation coefficient (R^2) to one. As the network's output increases, the chance of success also increases which is the aim of a model of this type. Clearly the network is producing reasonable results so it can be used to form the weights for the computer model.

It is possible to de-compile the network and extract the weights linking the inputs to the output. In this case it is a straightforward procedure because the network does not have a hidden layer, more complex networks are far more difficult to de-compile, and in fact complete PhD theses have been devoted to this subject. The following table shows the weights associated with the trained network given in Figure 1.

Figure 3 : Weights for the 7-Input Neural Network

Input	Weight	% Influence
Weight Carried	0.91	13.7%
Runners	-2.86	43.1%
Age	-0.28	4.2%
Days	-0.86	13.0%
Latest Race Form	-1.28	19.3%
Second Recent Race Form	-0.35	5.3%
Third Recent Race Form	-0.09	1.4%

Since the input values are normalised to the zero to one range the most influential input is the one with the largest weight, in absolute terms. From Figure 3 it can be seen that the *Runners* input has the largest absolute weight at -2.86. The fact that the weight is negative indicates that as the magnitude of this input increases, the output of the network reduces. In other words the chance of a horse winning reduces as the field size increases, which is not an unreasonable conclusion. However, since this input relates to the race as opposed to individual horses its effect will be the same for each runner in a race, so on a race-by-race basis its impact is irrelevant. This comment also applies to any race-related input which remains constant for each runner.

Figure 4: Success Rates in Non-Juvenile Turf Handicaps by Weight Band

Weight Carried	Wins	Runs	Wins%	Average Return/£1
10-01+	159	1906	8.3%	-£0.25
9-8 ..10-00	812	9292	8.7%	-£0.30
9-0 .. 9-07	1046	13605	7.7%	-£0.32
8-8 .. 8-13	936	13002	7.2%	-£0.29
8-0 .. 8-07	670	10452	6.4%	-£0.30
7-13	332	6873	4.8%	-£0.34

Weight Carried has a positive figure associated with it. Consequently as the weight the horse is set to carry increases the likelihood of success increases. Clearly carrying more weight does not improve the chance of a horse winning, but in general the horses near the top of the weights tend to win more often (see Figure 4), a feature which has been correctly identified by the network.

In terms of recent form, the latest race has most influence, almost four times the impact of the second most recent race. Going back three races appears to be irrelevant given the level of impact this input has on the outcome of the model. Course absence appears to be worth considering, though based on these findings it is not as important as the finishing position of the hose on its most recent run since the weight of the latter input is almost one-and-a-half times the weight of the *Days* variable.

Now that the importance of the variables has been established it is a simple matter to code the weights into the computerised model, though the values used by the program need to be normalised in the same way as they were for the network. At this stage it is often queried whether this step is relevant. Why bother transferring the weights to a second model when the network can be used just as well? Whilst it is true that the network will generate identical outputs to the computer program which uses its weights, networks are not particularly easy to interrogate in order to generate further explanation or information. These tasks are more easily handled by conventional programs so the resultant hybrid system should be easier to implement and run on a daily basis.

Often models of this type use an estimate of the starting price to improve their forecasting ability. Since the starting price is very highly correlated with the race result (i.e. the shorter the price the more likely the horse is to win) including such an input dramatically improves the accuracy of the model in terms of success rate. However, it should be noted that this does not guarantee bigger profits.

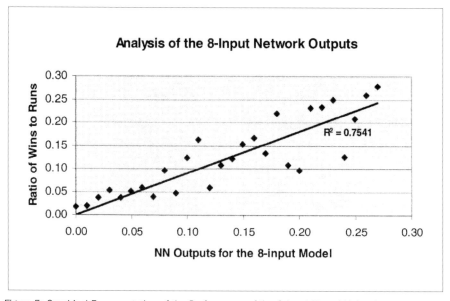

Figure 5: Graphical Representation of the Performance of the 8-Input Neural Network

Using the original data representation and including an eighth input which represents the starting price, an eight input neural network with one output was trained on 5,000 example cases and tested on a further 4,000 cases. The results of the test are given in Figure 5.

Again the network appears to perform well with a high correlation between the output of the network and the chance of success. The weights created by this network are given in

Figure 6.

Figure 6 : Weights for the 8-Input Neural Network

Input	Weight	% Influence
Starting Price	-19.29	90.2%
Weight Carried	-0.57	2.7%
Runners	-0.64	3.0%
Age	-0.39	1.8%
Days	0.24	1.1%
Latest Race Form	-0.22	1.0%
Second Recent Race Form	-0.01	0.0%
Third Recent Race Form	0.03	0.1%

The weights for this network are markedly different from the 7-input model. The most significant factor is the weight associated with the starting price. This input accounts for over 90% of the inputs' influence on the output and effectively renders the remaining variables insignificant. This is due to the high level of correlation between the starting price and chance of success.

Interestingly the *Days* variable now has a positive weight. In other words as the number of days the horse has been absent from the course increases the higher the success rate will be. This is purely due to the introduction of the starting price input and implies that the starting price for horses over-estimates the influence of the course absence.

The influence of the weight carried input has also changed sign. In this network horses with more weight will have their chance of success reduced. Again this is due to the impact of the price variable and implies that the bias of this input is too greatly skewed towards the higher weighted horses.

In order to generate an output for a horse it is necessary to establish the inputs then scale these by the weights derived from the network. So in the case of last race form, once this has been determined and scaled to the zero to one range, it is multiplied by the weight for this feature which is either -1.28 using the first set of weights, or -0.22 if the second structure is chosen. Using these two sets of weights the optimum horse can be easily defined. For the first set the horse that produces the highest output would have the following characteristics (ignoring the field size input):

Weight Allocated: 10-00
Age: three-year-old
Days Since Last Run: 1
Last three Form Figures: 111

For the second case the optimum horse would be characterised by the following attributes:

Weight Allocated: 7-12
Age: three-year-old
Days since Last run: 200
Last Three Form Figures: 011
Starting Price: 1/33

The difference between the two optimal horses is quite significant. This is due to the structure change between the two models resulting from the introduction of the starting price input which illustrates that the importance of each input is influenced by the other inputs that are used in the model. In the two examples given, the impact of the inputs not only changes in magnitude but also in direction. For instance, the introduction of new variables can reverse the influence of existing inputs. Consequently if new variables are to be added to an existing model it is necessary to recalculate the weights for all inputs.

Summary

The most critical phase in the development of a traditional computer-based forecasting model is the calculation of the weights which are applied to the input variables. If these weights are inaccurate with respect to the influence of the variables then the model will under-perform.

This article attempts to illustrate a new method for generating these weights which should ensure that the model performs to the limit of its expectations. However, even with optimal weights it is not guaranteed that the model will accurately forecast the results of horseraces. The performance of models of this type is also dependent on the choice of inputs and their representation. If these critical areas of system development are undertaken with care and rigour when combined with accurate weights the final model should possess a high degree of forecasting accuracy and become a helpful tool to the race analyst.

CHAPTER 2
ESTIMATING ABILITY USING DYNAMIC FORECASTING MODELS

Apparently it takes more than one Swallow to make a Summer, it certainly takes more than one race to accurately assess the ability of a horse. And yet many ratings compilers use just a single result to generate an assessment of ability.

Horses are assessed by ratings compilers, or Handicappers, each time they run. These assessments are normally referred to as performance ratings from which a Master Rating is determined. Since this figure will be associated with the horse for its next start it is of critical importance for race analysts who rely on ratings to determine the relative merits of the competing horses.

However, often this Master Rating is simply taken to be the best figure the horse has produced in recent performances. For instance, some Handicappers use the best rating the horse has achieved over its last three starts, others take a wider view examining the last six runs of a horse, whilst some retain the highest figure the animal has run to during the past two seasons. In each case the final assessment is based on a single race.

Whilst this approach can be justified, it does mean that a significant amount of information relating to the ability of the horse is completely ignored. Furthermore it places a great deal of weight on a single performance which is far from certain to be accurate. For example, when considering the conventional approach to speed figure compilation, there are several aspects of the calculation which are subject to error. The most basic of which is the standard time. Though based on previous race times, this figure is an estimate and consequently subject to error.

The going allowance, calculated to deduce the overall track speed, is another estimate that will often be inaccurate with slower run races during the afternoon making a single performance in a race run at a true pace appear to be far better than it really is. And, unfortunately, even the base data are subject to error. In Great Britain race times, until very recently, were hand-timed, leading to additional error, and with running rails moved on a regular basis it is not even possible to be confident about the actual race distance. With all of these possible errors creeping into calculations using a single race figure as the estimate of the animal's ability is not a particularly valid approach.

An alternative method is to simply take an average of the individual race ratings. So, for example, a horse which had raced three times and recorded the following figures 104 106 108, would be assigned a Master Figure of 106 using the arithmetic mean as the average. The main advantage of this approach is that it uses all the available information, as opposed to isolating a single item of data.

But there are some drawbacks as well. For instance the method does not account for possibly improving horses, these will always be undervalued. In the previous example, based on the three ratings the animal would appear to be improving, in which case setting the Master Figure at the mean level would, in all probability, under estimate the true level of ability. Another problem arises when a horse has won a race very easily, or has been eased towards the end of a race. The figures relating to these races will certainly under estimate the ability of the runner and using the averaging approach will have a negative impact on the final figure by reducing the mean value and, as a consequence, the Master Rating.

Furthermore, this method does not take into account the varying race conditions. In British racing horses run over different race distances and on different ground conditions which can affect the ability of the horse to produce its best rating. In the previous example the horse may not have been improving, instead the higher ratings may be due to different race conditions, such as a longer race distance or softer going. These elements need to be incorporated into any procedure designed to estimate the true ability of a horse, so a more sophisticated approach than a simple average is required.

A Distance Measure

It is reasonable to assume that a horse is more likely to reproduce an historical rating when the race conditions are similar. And that the likelihood of a horse running to a specific level reduces the more different the races conditions become. For example, a horse running over 3m4f is more likely to run to a rating previously recorded for races run over three miles and further rather than a rating recorded for a two-mile race. In order to use this in an alternative approach to generating a Master Rating it is first necessary to define a measure that will describe the differences between two races with respect to the key factors such as race distance, going and track configuration.

The simplest method is to use a standard distance measure that compares two races and generates a numerical value which represents their degree of similarity. Though this, at first, may appear to be complex, it is a very straightforward procedure that is easily implemented in any computer system.

Consider just two race conditions: the distance and the going. For Jumps racing the minimum race distance is 2 miles (excluding National Hunt Flat races) and the maximum is four-and-a-half miles. However, the bulk of races are run at distances between the minimum an 3 miles 2 furlongs. The going ranges from hard, the driest conditions, to heavy, the softest going on which racing is staged. Essentially there are seven discrete categories: hard, firm, good to firm, good, good to soft, soft and heavy. Before two races can be compared it is necessary to convert these factors to a new scale ranging from zero to one. For the race distance factor this means that a 2 mile race would map to zero and a 3m2f (or further) race would map to one. The equation that performs this mapping is given next:

New Distance Scale = (Race Distance (f) - 16)/10 if race distance <= 26F, otherwise 1

Using this conversion 2 mile (or 16 furlongs) races map to 0, 2 mile 4f (20 furlongs) races map to 0.4 and so on. Any race distance of 3m2f or further maps to one. For the going factor the seven categories can be converted to a simple numeric scale [1-7] then a similar procedure to the race distance used to perform the mapping. So hard going would map to 0, good going (the centre point of the scale) would map to 0.5, and heavy going would map to 1. Naturally this approach does assume and equal distance between the going categories and this may be adjusted if it is thought necessary. For instance the technique assumes an equal distance between the categories good and good to soft, and between soft and heavy. Given that the heavy going category is the softest ground that can be encountered it may be beneficial to widen the distance between these two groups.

When graphed, the space formed by these two factors is a square with each race lying within its boundaries. Comparing two races is a simple matter of placing them in the square (i.e. determining their co-ordinates by using the above scaling procedures) then calculating the distance between them. For example, consider the following two races:

Race A: 2 miles, hard going
Race B: 3 miles 2 furlongs, heavy ground.

The races are shown on the graph together with a two other races. Race A is over the minimum distance and on the driest ground, consequently its position on the graph is at the lower left-hand corner (relating to the co-ordinate (0,0)). Race B is the other extreme and as a result is diametrically opposed to Race A. From the graph it can be seen that the distance between the two races, A and B, is the maximum it can be, stretching across the diagonal of the square. This is not surprising given the characteristics of the two events and the fact that they are described by the maximum and minimum values of the new scales.

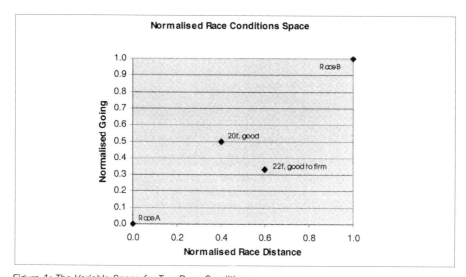

Figure 1: The Variable Space for Two Race Conditions

Determining the distance between two races is a straightforward procedure using the race co-ordinates and Pythagoras' theorem. For the two races, A and B, the distance between them can be calculated as follows:

$$\sqrt{[(1-0)^2 + (1-0)^2} = \sqrt{2} \approx 1.4$$

The co-ordinates of the other two races given in the graph are: (0.4,0.5) and (0.6,0.33), representing a 2 mile 4 furlong race on good ground and a 2 mile 6 furlong race on good to firm ground. Calculating the distance between these two events results in:

$$\sqrt{[(0.4-0.6)^2 + (0.5-0.33)^2]} = \sqrt{0.07} \approx 0.26$$

Clearly these two races are closer in terms of race conditions than races A and B which is illustrated by the lower distance measure as well as their relative positions on the graph.

In these examples only two race conditions are considered (race distance and going) but the method can be applied to any number of factors. Adding a third variable simply converts the space from a square into a cube. The method of calculation remains as above, though a third component is added representing the third co-ordinate. The general form is given by:

$$\text{Distance} \quad \sqrt{\sum_{r=1}^{n} (x_r - y_r)^2} \quad \text{for spaces with } n \text{ dimensions}$$

Using the Distance Measure to Forecast Ability

Before applying this technique to the ratings it is necessary to define which race factors will be used in the comparison. Naturally race distance and going need to be included, and for National Hunt racing track direction could be added along with track configuration in terms of stiff, undulating or flat.

One other factor which needs to be considered is time. Though this is not related to race conditions it has a bearing on the ratings forecast. A horse is more likely to run to the level achieved in recent races than earlier it its career. For instance a recent run on heavy ground is a better guide to the ability of the runner than a performance on the same surface recorded four years ago. Similarly horses tend to stay longer distances as they age, consequently a run over three miles several years ago should have lower impact on the assessment of ability than a recent run over the same distance simply because the horse may not have had sufficient stamina when first tried over the distance but as an older animal it is now stronger and more able to stay the distance. The time variable can be added as a simple weight or incorporated into the distance measure.

Once the factors have been determined, forecasting the performance rating is a matter of calculating a weighted average using the distance measure as the weight. The closer two races are the greater the weight should be, thus giving the race rating more impact on the final figure. However, the closer races are to each other the lower the distance measure will be. So simply using the distance would reduce the impact of close races as opposed to increasing it. To solve this problem it is necessary to use the reciprocal of the distance as the weight.

As an example, consider the two races, A and B, described before with the following performance ratings:

Figure 2: Example Race Conditions

Race Identification	Distance	Going	Rating Achieved
Race A	2 miles	Hard	100
Race B	3 miles 2 furlongs	Heavy	20

Clearly the horse is better when less emphasis is placed on stamina since he recorded his best rating, 100, over the minimum distance and on hard going, whereas his performance over further on heavy ground was exceptionally poor.

If the next race the horse is due to contest is similar to Race A (i.e. 2 miles hard going) the forecast rating becomes:

$$\text{Forecast Rating} = \frac{(100 \times w_1 + 20 \times w_2)}{(w_1 + w_2)}$$

where w_1 and w_2 are the weights derived for each race as follows:

$$w_1 = \frac{1}{(1 + dm(A))} \text{ and } w_2 = \frac{1}{(1 + dm(B))}$$

where dm(A) denotes the distance between the next race and race A. The additional "1" in the denominator is to prevent division by zero which would happen with two identical races.

In this example $w_1 = 1/(1+0) = 1$, and $w_2 = 1/(1+1.4) = 0.414$ therefore:

$$\text{Forecast Rating} = \frac{(100 + 20 \times 0.414)}{1.414} \approx 77$$

If the next race in which the horse is due to run is similar to Race B (i.e. 3 miles 2 furlongs, heavy going), then using the same method the forecast rating becomes 43. Naturally the horse is forecast to return a higher rating when the race conditions are less demanding, which is a reasonable assumption given the historical ratings achieved.

The main benefit of this approach is that it does not employ fixed weights for different conditions and instead derives the level of influence of the variables from the historical cases. In this respect it may be considered to be a dynamic approach since it does not use fixed constants for each horse. Consequently the model is horse specific and not a general model that can be applied to any runner. In other words it is based on data for a particular horse as opposed to data collected from all runners.

Although the method reflects the impact of the race conditions on each horse when generating the ability rating, it does assume equal influence for each of the variables used. For instance, in the previous example the race distance and going are given equal weight in the calculation. This may be suitable for many variables, but possibly not for all. Other variables such as track direction may have less overall influence. Naturally additional weighting could be introduced to make the necessary adjustment. However, a simpler approach is to adjust the scale of the variables.

For three variables with equal influence, the method needs to determine the distances between the races in three dimensions. A graphical representation of this would be a cube. To reduce the influence of one of the variables such as the track direction, the scale could be reduced with left-handed tracks indicated by a zero, and right-handed tracks represented by 0.5 as opposed to one. The effect is to move the two options closer together, reduce the total volume of the variable space and give this variable less influence on the distance measure. Such a move modifies the variable space, changing the cube into a cuboid. The method of calculation stays the same, but the results are different. However, this does assume some knowledge of the relative influence of each of the variables, which may not be entirely valid and more accurate methods are preferred.

The Neural Network Approach

The distance measure introduced in the previous section can be used as a dynamic forecasting method for predicting ability ratings under varying race conditions. However, the variables need to be treated equally, or arbitrary weights in the form of scale changes need to be introduced. An alternative solution is to adopt an approach that retains the dynamic form of the distance method but also introduces a suitable weighting process to compensate for the varying levels of influence of the race conditions.

A multiple regression model is a possible solution or, preferably, a neural network. The main drawback associated with either approach is the lack of data. Horses do not run that often so the training data (the data on which the model is based) will not be particularly extensive. Normally with a neural network approach the data set would be divided into three partitions to be used separately for training, testing and validation. However, given the lack of data that approach is not practical for this problem. Whilst a hold-one-out method can be used, for this application training used the complete set and continued until the error measure stopped decreasing. Although this approach uses all of the available data, the number of training cases is still very small and as such the network should have very few hidden nodes, maybe two or three only, depending on the number on inputs considered. As an example consider the handicap hurdler Tilty.

Figure 3: Historical Race Performances for Tilty

Race Distance	Going	Days since last run	Course Direction	Rating Achieved
24.5	good	29	L-H	104
26	good to soft	54	R-H	104
26.5	soft	35	R-H	68
25.5	good	13	L-H	99
26	good to soft	7	R-H	99
26	good	11	R-H	99
26	soft	25	R-H	96
24.5	soft	19	R-H	51
26.5	good to soft	27	R-H	97
25.5	good	33	L-H	97

The data given in Figure 3 can be used to train a neural network to predict the rating the horse is likely to achieve on its next start. For instance given the race conditions: 2 mile 4 furlong race, good going, 41 days since last run, and left-handed course, the network predicts that Tilty would record a rating of 90. This process of training the network then applying it to today's race conditions would be followed for each runner in the race to generate a set of ratings that could be used to rank the runners.

Analysing the structure of the individual networks can also be informative. In this case, keeping the race distance, days since last run, and course direction fixed at 25f, 20 days and right-handed but allowing the going to vary over the seven categories the following forecast ratings are generated:

Prevailing Going	Predicted Rating
good to firm	109
good	98
good to soft	85
soft	71
heavy	58

Clearly from this analysis Tilty is better suited by fast going than soft. Interestingly changing the course direction to left-handed reduced the ratings by about 3 points, in this case, but changing the days since last run input made no significance difference to the figures.

Summary

A dynamic forecasting approach offers a powerful solution to the problem of determining the master rating for a horse. However, this method is not restricted to ratings and can be used to predict a whole range of variables. For example, the target variable, formerly the master rating, could be replaced by a race performance indicator with the model used to predict whether a horse is likely to run well under the specific race conditions. This type of model could be used to highlight short-priced horses that are unlikely to run to form. The main drawback concerns the lack of data, but providing the model does not over-fit the training cases the results should be valid.

CHAPTER 3
NEURAL NETWORKS, LEARNING METHODS
AND ALL WEATHER RACING

If artificial neural networks are good at anything it is generating mappings and finding relationships between sets of data. For instance, given the heights, waist measurements and body weights of several people, a neural network could determine a relationship between these data that would map the height and waist data to the body weight. This relationship could then be used to predict the weight of other people that did not form part of the initial data set. In this example the relationship is likely to be quite simple, and probably linear, though a neural network can equally find more complex mappings.

In order to create the mapping, the network compares each input pattern (height and waist size for example) with the required output, which for this example is body weight. Given a set of training patterns, or example cases, depending on the terminology preferred, the network will make several passes through the sample and generate a mapping which links the input data to the output. This process is often referred to as learning since it mirrors the way we believe humans, especially children, learn specific knowledge.

Essentially children learn by example. Repeat to a child that $1+1= 2$ several thousand times and he/she will eventually associate $1+1$ with the answer 2. The child may not have any understanding of what "1" or "+" or "2" actually mean in the real world but he/she knows that given the input pattern, or query, "$1+1$" then the required output, or reply, is "2".

Equally the child could be told that $1+1=10$ and that $2+2=100$ and so on, and would learn this new relationship probably without questioning its validity. A neural network could also be taught such a mapping. In this specific case there is a degree of logic in the approach but other less valid training patterns can also be fed into a network which will happily derive a relationship. For example, a network would have no problems finding a mapping for the following training patterns:

$$1+1=10,\ 2+2=8,\ 3+3=6,\ 4+4=4,\ 5+5=2,\ 6+6=0$$

The mapping will be correct for the given training cases but would be far from useful. It is important to note here that the network has no understanding of "+" and in the first case would only be given the input pattern $(1,1)$ with the associated output 10.

This lack of prior knowledge about the problem can be beneficial, it can also lead to unexpected results. Taking a horseracing example, it is possible to express the likelihood of success for a single horse as a rating based on such factors as going and distance suitability. To create this rating, points could be assigned for each of the factors, such 10 points for a horse suited by the going and 8 for a horse suited by the race distance. Consequently, a horse suited by both the going and race distance would be assigned an initial rating of 10+8=18. However, the network may take a different view and its equivalent to "10+8" may not equal 18. It is possible that this simple addition of the two values may not be the best approach and the network may have found a more reliable mapping.

This is the main power of neural networks. Even with no previous knowledge or understanding of the problem they will generate a valid solution based on the example cases with which they are presented. The weakness is that the outcome depends to such a great extent on the training data and the way it is represented. Therefore it is of critical importance that the data fully represents the domain and is encoded in an acceptable way.

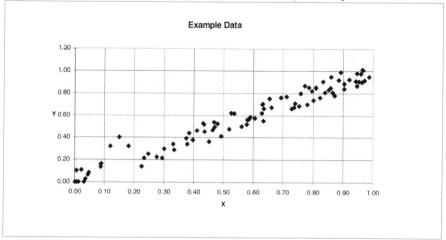

Figure 1: Example Data. These data would be represented by a one input model with one output node

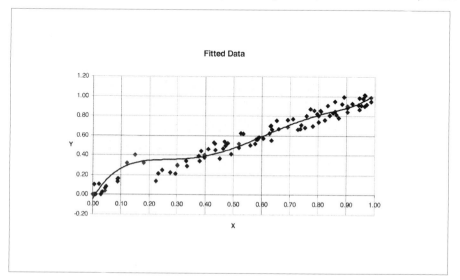

Figure 2: Fitted Data. The network function is indicated by the solid line and has attempted to map all of the points including the outliers which has resulted in a deviation from the underlying linear trend.

This immense power at finding mappings can also present problems. There are cases where the network can be over-trained. For example consider the data in Figure 1. It would not take a network long to generate the mapping given in Figure 2. This new function maps the input values (x) to the outputs values (y) extremely well with only minimal variation throughout. But is it the best mapping? Mathematically it probably is the most accurate mapping but practically it probably isn't. Looking at the data it can be seen that there is a linear relationship between the inputs and the outputs. In general as one increases so does the other, apart from a few cases near the origin. So the underlying relationship is probably linear and not a complex non-linear form as indicated in Figure 2. In this case the network would be considered to be over-trained: It has tried to justify every training pattern within the mapping whether they are outliers, or more simply, erroneous cases, but in doing so has lost sight of the overall association between the data.

Humans are also guilty of this process. How many racing systems have you come across that have stipulated very precise rules that require several conditions to be met before a selection can be found? For example when considering the horses drawn in stall one at a certain racecourse over 1 mile the following table (Figure 3) may be generated:

Number Of Runners	Average Return/£1
2	0.07
3	0.09
4	0.08
5	0.09
6	0.11
7	0.12
8	0.13
9	-0.15
10	0.10
11	0.18
12	0.13

Figure 3: Example Data. The return is given as profit per £1 staked for horses drawn in stall one. A negative figure indicates a loss, a return of 0.09 would be required to cover the old off-course betting tax at 9%.

A system could be structured to back the horse drawn in stall one unless there are nine runners in the race and to double the stake if there are 11 runners. There is no real justification for the statement, expect from the limited amount of data available which, in all probability, do not reflect the true underlying trend.

Consequently it is important to understand the data, and the likely relationships, before training the network. If the system is likely to be linear then omit the hidden layer of the network and train a linear system, this will avoid over-training. Also once the network has been trained it is a good idea to plot the outputs for example cases in order to get an understanding of how the mapping works, and whether it is reasonable. Alternatively it is possible to generate measures of input variable influence and check for validity.

Case Study – All Weather Handicaps

Clearly there is no best way to construct a neural network. To demonstrate one possible approach this section uses all weather handicaps to provide a framework for analysing the various stages involved in designing and implementing a network.

As with most model building projects, the first stage is data collection. For this problem it is a matter of generating a set of data relating to all weather handicaps which includes all of the variables that are considered to make a worthwhile contribution to the network. At this point though consideration should be given to how the network will be used once implemented. If it requires all future data (when it is live running) to be input manually having a network with 425 inputs covering every aspect of all weather racing will be difficult to use for obvious reasons. Naturally if the data are to be made available from some other computer system already in place the number of inputs will only affect the speed of training.

Since this network will require manual input the number of inputs has been restricted to the following:
* *number of runners in the race*
* *track identification*
* *ratings of five highest rated horses*
* *weight carried by five highest rated horses*
* *prices of the five highest rated horses*

The outputs are:
* *return from backing the top-rated horse to win*
* *return from backing the top-rated horse each way*
* *return from backing the second-top rated horse to win*
* *return from backing the second-top-rated horse each way*
* *CSF from backing the top two rated horses*
* *reverse CSF for the top two rated horses*
* *reverse CSF from backing the top three rated horses*

The aim of the network is to determine the best betting strategy from the various options, for instance a win bet, or a reverse forecast.

We are now faced with probably the most important phase of neural network development: data representation. For new users of neural networks it is strongly recommended that simple problems are tested with different data representations and the networks' performance validated in terms of accuracy, speed of training, and type of mapping.

For this problem the track identification is allocated three inputs, set to either 1 or 0, to represent the three different tracks. For instance Lingfield is represented as 1 0 0 in the input pattern. The other variables are all represented as real inputs. However, the ratings are input as differences from the top-rated horse. In other words given five horses rated 75, 72, 68, 66, and 50 the ratings of only the last four would be put into the network as 3, 7, 9, and 25 (i.e. 75-72, 75-68,...).

One major problem with this type of data is setting the upper and lower bounds of each input. Ratings can vary from 0 to 140, starting price from 0 to 500 and a CSF return from -1 to 1000+. Limits have to be set since the inputs need to be mapped to the [0,1] or [-1,1] space (i.e. networks will only accept values in the -1 to 1 range). Although it is a simple matter to fix these values it is important to realise what this will actually do to the data from which the network will learn. For instance the majority of values for the CSF will be -1 representing a losing bet. However, there will be some high returns so setting a large upper limit, say 500, condenses the values into a [0,1] range but clusters them all towards the lower end. Since this term is to be used a an output and will be compared to the value generated by the network to determine an error function (how well the network has mapped the data sets) if the network simply generated a value of -1 for every case the error function would be very small due to this clustering. This needs to be addressed in the training phase, or alternatively by representing the variable as four different output nodes each assigned a range of possible CSF values (i.e. -1, 0..10, 11..100, 100+).

Once the representation has been decided the data set can be divided into three sets: training data, testing data and validation data. The training set is used to create the network whilst the test data can be used to monitor its performance against other networks. The validation set is used as a final check of the most suitable network.

Before training is initiated there is another issue to be addressed: the number of hidden nodes in the network. Unfortunately there is no straightforward answer to the "how many hidden nodes should be used?" question, it really depends on the complexity of the problem. If it is thought that a linear solution would be adequate then set the number to zero and train a linear network. Alternatively, for non-linear systems a good policy is to start with a minimum number of hidden nodes, perhaps two or even zero, train and test the network then increase the number of hidden nodes and retrain. A process of doubling the number of hidden node followed by training and testing can then be initiated until a suitable network is created. This network can then be finally tested against the validation set.

Network Output	Number of Cases	Average Return From the Validation Set
Any Value	100	0.01
0 and higher	48	0.12
0.1 and higher	43	0.25
0.2 and higher	37	0.27
0.3 and higher	29	0.62
0.4 and higher	24	0.77
0.5 and higher	17	1.03
0.6 and higher	14	0.79
0.7 and higher	9	0.22

Figure 4: Results Table. To generate the results a threshold approach was adopted. Consequently all cases with a neural network output value above specific thresholds from 0 to 0.7 were recorded.

For the all weather problem several networks were trained and tested and the following results given in Figure 4 were obtained for the Top-Rated to Win output from the best network. It should be noted that the output of the network is the expected profit from the bet and can range from -1 (indicating that all training cases in the neighbourhood of the test case were losers) to the highest winning price used in the training. In reality it ranges from -0.48 to 1.01 where a value of 0.09 would represent the break-even point for betting off-course and paying 9% tax.

From Figure 4 it can be seen that for all cases in the validation set a profit would have been made from simply backing the top rated to win (1p per £1 in fact). However, by just considering those with a network output value of 0 or higher increases the return to 12p/£1 for the validation cases, and for those with a network value of 0.4 or higher improves the profit to 77p/£1.

These results are quite encouraging and suggest that a profit would be made from following the advice of the network. However, the output of the network is arrived at after an amount of work such as inputting all the necessary data, so a question that needs to be asked is whether the network adds sufficient value to the all weather ratings to make the additional work worthwhile.

From an analysis of the data for the 2000 season (from which the neural network data was extracted) the following features can be identified. Backing all top-rated horses in all weather handicaps would have produced a profit of £23.44 from 353 bets (7p/£1), but by considering just those with a minimum rating value of 20 from their last three races (an example of the ratings for a particular race is given in Figure 5) increases the return to £47.42 from 240 bets (20p/£1) and this requires no further effort since the last three ratings form part of the daily ratings summary. In fact adjusting this lower limit can give excellent returns as demonstrated graphically in Figure 6.

Lingfield 19 January 2000 – 12.0f Handicap – 2.40 Class C

Horse	Draw	99	3rd	2nd	1st	00	MFig
QUINTRELL DOWNS	(2)	10^2S	102^1S	56^3W	85^2S	0	96
SPACE RACE	(4)	95L	0^0L	61^2L	106^1L	106L	95
NOUKARI	(1)	109L	72^1L	28^4L	92^2L	92L	85
PUZZLEMENT	(7)	84L	73^9W	84^4L	76^5L	0	81
CHINA CASTLE	(3)	98W	57^2L	53^5W	30^4L	0	69
RAYIK	(5)	96W	44^0L	0^6W	44^7L	0	61
RANDOM KINDNESS	(6)	59W	0	0	59^7W	0	58

Figure 5: Ratings Example. This example shows the ratings for the last three runs for each horse, the finishing position in each race (superscript) and the course identification (S, L, or W). The following key is also used for the columns: today's draw position, best rating of 1999; third most recent rating; second most recent rating; most recent rating; best rating of 2000 season; and master rating.

For the race in Figure 5 the top-rated horse, Quintrell Downs, has a master figure of 96. The lowest figure Quintrell Downs has recorded over his last three starts was 56, consequently this is the type of runner that would be expected to return a profit in the long run.

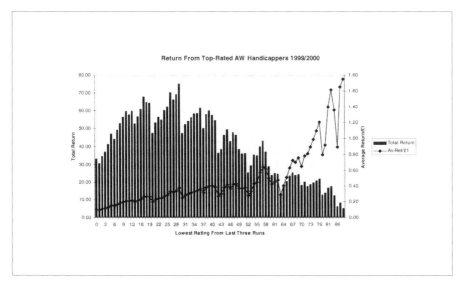

Figure 6: Returns Graph. From this graph it can be seen that in general the return per bet increases as the lower limit imposed on the last three ratings increases. However, the total return reaches a maximum earlier then declines which is due to the reduction in the number of bets as the lower limit increases.

Consequently for this problem it is not necessary to use a neural network since a simple graphical analysis can provide the necessary information to form a profitable betting strategy. This will not always be the case though since it depends on the complexity of the problem and the importance of the individual variables under consideration. However, simply because neural networks offer convenient solutions to these problems does not necessarily mean they will provide the most effective answer.